The S.E.L.L. System™

A comprehensive guide to success
in marketing and selling for new
and small businesses

Lynne Thomas

Lynne Thomas

DEDICATION

This book is dedicated to my wonderful partner Ian who has always been there to encourage me in my dreams, no matter how hair-brained they may have seemed at the time, my business buddy Lisa Simcox for encouraging me to write it and giving me the benefit of her extensive marketing experience and to my son Chris who designed the cover and internal images. Without their encouragement and support this book would never have seen the light of day.

Contents

Lynne Thomas

ACKNOWLEDGMENTS

My sincere thanks to Lisa M Billingham for her guidance and expert support in helping me with the technicalities of publishing this book. My eternal gratitude to the wonderful small business owners who've put their trust in me over the years and without who's support The S.E.L.L. System™ could never have been created.

Introduction

I would like to start this book by sharing a little secret with you. I didn't want to write a bloomin' book. In fact, I managed to dodge it for about 5 years until my business bestie got all up in my face and told me that it would be a great way for those who can't afford to work with me on a one-to-one basis to access my system. As this fits in with my vision of "more wealth for everyone" and made my methodology accessible to all, I acquiesced - and here we are.

Another thing I would like to share with you is that although this book is called The S.E.L.L. System it is not really about selling – although of course that does get mentioned a few times. S.E.L.L. is an acronym and stands for Stand Out, Engage, Leverage and Level Up, and if you do these 4 things in your business you shouldn't need to do much selling, as your marketing and current customers will do it all for you, and I don't know about you, but I think that's a much better way of doing business.

Okay, are you ready to sell more things to more people more of the time? Great, grab a cuppa and settle down as this book is going to share the EXACT strategies that my clients and I use to build, grow and scale our businesses.

Welcome to my book – The S.E.L.L. System™ - where I talk you through the 4 simple steps you need to take as a business owner to get top quality leads rolling in, customers queuing up to work with you and evangelists and cheerleaders shouting your name from the roof tops as the best person to buy from. These steps are not difficult. They do not require any specific skill set that a savvy entrepreneur such as yourself wouldn't already possess and they don't take years to work, just in case you were wondering. In fact, I follow these exact 4 steps with my one-to-one clients, and we get results in just 4 weeks!

So, why is this system any different to any of the other thousand systems that you've no doubt come across? Well, I'll let you decide that for yourself as you read through the pages of this book, but I will say this, I have used this method (or a version of it) in all kinds of businesses both on and offline, service based and product based in the UK and all around the world, and to put it simply – it works. Okay, I'm going to say that aren't I, but I've included some great testimonials in the book to illustrate what others who've gone before you have achieved when they've followed this simple formula.

Here's one from Matthew. He has an extraordinarily niched

business and didn't think my methods would work for him. His company produce bread baskets which they make on 3D printers for the likes of Greggs and Asda, and he had tried all kinds of things to get the product noticed by his ideal customer, but to no avail.

I first met Matthew when he attended one of my marketing masterclasses. He wanted to know if there was something else he could do to get his bread baskets out into the world where they would be noticed and snapped up by those who use them. After doing just ONE of the things I suggested this is what happened…

Matthew Bowdler
21 day straight sales!
This is a company new for us, it came to an end this week but we know that we can achieve it.
So here's to the next run!

Like · Reply · 14 m

Lynne Thomas ⊙ Author
That's amazing Matthew. Well done and congratulations 🥂 ✓ Here's to the next run too!

So, there you are, the first example of how powerful this method can be if you apply it in your business as I outline it in the following pages.

I guess I should start with a little introduction. "Oh no," I hear you cry, "Not 45 pages of waffle about what you've done for the last however many years, can't we just skip to the juicy bits?" Yep, we can do that instead, and if you're interested to learn more about me you can read it in the blurb at the end, how's about that?

Okay, so let's get into the juicy bits and start to look at how you can quickly and easily turn things around in your business if you have the will, the determination and the drive. "WHAAAT??? I thought this was supposed to be 4 *simple* steps!"

Although the steps are simple, they do require some work to get them set up and running like clockwork, but once you've done that you can sit back and reap the endless rewards of your labour. And by the way, I'm English and I write in UK English so yes, labour does have a U in it.

My vision for this book is that it acts as a mentor and guide to help you get the most out of your marketing so that you attract more clients and make more sales. I can't work with everyone as I have limited capacity for one-to-one clients, but I *want* to work with everyone, so I'm writing this book in the hope that it will be the next best thing to having me right there with you.

My intentions for the book are simple. I intend to give you all the information you need to create unbeatable sales and marketing strategies by providing invaluable insights, proven techniques, and actionable strategies that will empower you to unleash your business's true potential. I also intend for this book to equip you with the tools to navigate the competitive marketplace and achieve unprecedented success.

My reason for writing this book is also simple (aside from my business bestie nagging away at me for months). I wanted to break down the intricacies of effective marketing and sales practices, offering practical advice, and highlighting real-world examples of businesses that have thrived using these strategies. By combining time-tested principles with innovative approaches, my aim is that this book delivers a comprehensive framework that ensures long-term growth and profitability. Just think of it as your ultimate roadmap to mastering the art of sales and marketing in this dynamic and ever-changing world of business.

Inside the pages of "The S.E.L.L. System™ " you'll discover:

1. The fundamentals of marketing: Learn how to define your target audience, craft a compelling brand story, and develop a powerful marketing plan that resonates with your customers.
2. Sales strategies that convert: Master the art of selling, from prospecting and lead generation to closing deals and nurturing long-term customer relationships.
3. Digital marketing domination: Unleash the potential of digital channels, including social media, content marketing, search engine optimisation (SEO), and email marketing, to drive customer engagement and boost your online presence.
4. Customer-centric approach: Understand your customers' needs, wants, and pain points, and create tailored solutions that solve their problems and exceed their expectations.

5. Scaling your business: Unlock the secrets to scaling your operations, expanding your market reach, and staying ahead of the competition while maintaining profitability.

Whether you're a novice entrepreneur or an experienced business owner, "The S.E.L.L. System™ " provides you with the essential knowledge and practical guidance needed to thrive in today's competitive marketplace and my hope is that you will take advantage of the advice and guidance given here and apply it faithfully to your business. Remember, this stuff only works if you put it into practice!

Okay, with all that said let's get started. The S.E.L.L. System™ is divided into 4 parts – so the book is too – just to keep things simple (I like simple).

Part One: Stand Out

Part One Introduction

In today's competitive business landscape, standing out from the crowd is crucial for small business owners, and with numerous entrepreneurs vying for customers' attention it's essential to differentiate yourself and leave a lasting impression. This introduction to Part One of the S.E.L.L. System™ will explore five effective strategies that can help business owners stand out among their competitors, ensuring long-term success and growth.

By the end of Part One you will know how to easily attract your ideal clients which is the first step of successful selling, but to prepare for this chapter you are going to need to think about the following:

- Your vision and mission
- Your ultimate goals

- What you are selling
- Who you are selling it to
- What your message is going to be
- How to deliver on the wow factor

Don't worry though, I am going to be talking you through each of these steps so that by the end of Part One of this book you will have it all covered off, which will make the next stage even easier.

It is also worth noting that I only teach what I do, and what I know works, so there may be other things you can try that will be even more effective at attracting your ideal clients and that is fine too – I hope to give you a flavour of what I mean by the term "standing out" by way of the examples of strategies I have chosen to include here.

1. **Develop a Unique Value Proposition** (in other words a compelling offer)

To stand out, you must clearly communicate your unique value proposition (UVP). Your Unique offer is what sets you apart from your competitors and answers the question, "Why should customers choose you?" Identify your strengths, key differentiators, and the specific benefits you offer. Craft a compelling message that resonates with your target audience, highlighting how your product or service solves their problems or fulfils their needs better than anyone else.

In simple English we are aiming to set ourselves apart from our competitors so that our ideal clients recognise that we can help them. To this end we must craft messaging that resonates with them and create an offer that they know they want.

For example: I am a business mentor, but a quick LinkedIn search reveals 216,000 business mentors are registered on LinkedIn and that's a lot of competition. Instead, I call myself The Business Builder and this narrows down the pool to just 4,300 of us.

By saying that I am the business builder I am also calling out to that specific audience – those that are looking to build, grow or scale a business and need help with systems, processes and strategies to enable them to do this successfully – this is a great start.

But I also need to make sure that I am speaking to them in the language they use and about things that they are interested in, concerned about or want answers to. By speaking directly to them about specific issues ensures my target audience will notice me, engage with me and, more importantly, buy from me.

A good example of this is when I use the word "strategy" in a phrase such as – I can help you sort out your social media strategy once and for all. The problem with this is that I've learned that my clients don't necessarily know what a "strategy" is, they refer to it as plan, therefore if I use the word plan, they are more likely to tune into what I'm saying and understand what I mean. I was also somewhat surprised to find out that many new business owners don't know what a "lead" is (it's someone who has shown an interest in what you are selling).

Here is my offer…

I help small business owners increase your turnover without having to increase your staff, financial investment or time in the office! I do this by helping you identify and plug gaps in your marketing and sales strategies where potential sales are slipping away un-noticed. By plugging these gaps, you can increase your turnover without having to increase your workload.

.

Now don't you think that's a far better way of saying that I'm a business mentor who can help with increasing your turnover?

2. Build a Strong Brand Identity

A strong and consistent brand identity is crucial for standing out in a crowded market. Develop a compelling brand story that connects emotionally with your customers. Create a memorable logo, choose a distinctive colour palette, and design a visually appealing website and marketing materials. Consistency across all touchpoints will make your brand recognisable and leave a lasting impression.

For example: You will see that I use a coral pink, mustard yellow and turquoise blue in my posts, on my website and in my images. This palette is consistent across everything I do both online and offline. It is used on my pull-up banner when I go to events, on my workbooks and notebooks that I send out to my clients and even in the images contained in this book.

But it's not just the colours and logo that are important, you need to get across your values too. Telling your business story helps people connect with your business in a way that they can't from a quick social media post that is shouting about your offer. You need to get to them on an emotional level and sharing your story with your audience is an extremely effective way of achieving this.

My story includes: how I accidentally fell into mentoring small business owners, how I struggled to get clients in the beginning, how I worked with some of the best online marketers in the world and how I ended up where I am today. I share my hopes, dreams, disasters, successes and also the things I've found along the way that have helped me grow my business such as tools and apps.

I am also clear about who I am as a person (coz I'm not everyone's cup of tea) I'm a bit too honest for some people and that's okay, there will be someone out there for them. I share my values (number 1 is fairness) and I am also not afraid to let people know when things don't go to plan – they seem to love hearing about that more than anything.

All of this is helping to develop my brand identity. People are getting to know the character of the business as well as my character. They are buying into me, which in turn means they are buying into my business and my brand. The Business Builder's brand is quirky and fun – we wanted to stand out from our competitors by leaving behind the corporate image that most coaches and mentors cling to and instead offer a fun and quirky alternative. Check out our website to see what I mean www.thebusinessbuilderonline.com

3. Provide Exceptional Customer Service

One sure-fire way to stand out is by delivering exceptional customer service. Go above and beyond to exceed your customers' expectations. Train your employees to be knowledgeable, courteous, and attentive to customer needs.

Actively listen to feedback and make improvements accordingly. By providing a personalised and positive experience, you'll differentiate yourself from competitors who offer a lacklustre service.

I often explain this to my clients as wowing and wooing their clients. How can you wow your audience so that they show an interest in you and once you have their attention how can you woo them to keep it. Think of it exactly like dating. First you have to do something to get noticed, then once you've been noticed and approached you need to woo the heck out of 'em until they surrender to your charms. Take them to a nice restaurant, show an interest in their favourite film or music, show up for their Karaoke night and make a point of LOVING their best friend.

In my business I offer lots of helpful hints, tips, suggestions, training videos, masterclasses and workshops to wow my potential clients. I give them amazingly insane value up front and often for free. Once I have their attention and they become a lead I woo them by giving them even more insane value – I offer a totally free 60-minute zoom call where I can help them put together a marketing blueprint for their specific business which is totally unique to them and that they can start implementing straight away – Like I said, insane value.

But when they become customers this wowing and wooing shouldn't cease. I send them a surprise welcome package to their home address with all kinds of goodies and helpful stuff inside on signing up with me. I go above and beyond what I promise to make sure my clients achieve their goals – and I usually end up having conversations with them way after their time with me has ended (which I don't charge for).

If you can think about all the opportunities you have to wow and woo your clients you will automatically stand out from your competitors who are mostly not doing this.

4. Leverage Digital Marketing Channels

In the digital age, an effective online presence is paramount. Invest in search engine optimisation (SEO) to improve your website's visibility in search engine results. Develop a content marketing strategy to provide valuable information to your target audience and establish yourself as an industry thought leader. Engage with customers through social media platforms, utilising creative and interactive campaigns. Embrace digital advertising, targeting specific demographics to maximise your reach. By utilising these channels strategically, you can attract and retain customers, standing out from your competition.

Well Duh! I know, who doesn't know about using digital marketing channels these days but let me tell you, I work with so many clients who are only making use of one or two of the available channels and therefore missing out on many opportunities to generate leads and make sales. For example, they may be on social media but not using email campaigns. The more visible you are the more chance your ideal client has of finding you and the better your chances of making a sale.

If you have a website, you absolutely need an SEO strategy to help you get found among the trillions of webpages out there. You need to think about the keywords you want to be ranked for and then make sure you have them in all the appropriate places on your website. But don't worry if you don't have a website, you can still rank on Google under Your Facebook or LinkedIn listing if you've used the right keywords in your headlines or bio.

For example: I want to rank for the term "The Business

Builder" because that is my niche (or ideal client) as this is one of the main services that I provide, and if you look for a The Business Builder in Worcester you will see me show up under my LinkedIn listing – which also includes the link to my website.

Social media is pretty much a given these days. You need some kind of social presence, but which channel you choose is entirely up to you. I, for instance, use LinkedIn as my chosen channel because that's where my ideal clients hang out – I no longer have a Facebook account (but that's another story) so that just goes to show that you don't need to be everywhere – just be in one or two places but show up regularly and have a plan for your content so that it generates leads for you that you can then convert into paying clients.

Google ads, Facebook ads and Microsoft ads are also a great way of attracting new business, but I would work with someone who knows what they are doing because you can lose loads of money and not achieve a single sale if you don't know how to set your ads up correctly or create copy that connects and converts. That said, if you want faster results this is definitely the way to go.

5.   Foster Innovation and Adaptability

To remain competitive, new business owners must embrace innovation and adapt to changing market trends. Stay abreast of the latest industry developments and technological advancements. Encourage creativity and forward-thinking within your business. Continually seek ways to improve your products, services, and processes. By being agile and responsive, you'll demonstrate your commitment to meeting customer needs in a rapidly evolving business landscape.

Again, in simple terms this just means stay one step ahead of your competitors. The more innovative you can be in your business the more attractive it becomes and the more clients you can win over. A good example of this is when I decided to offer tech support to my clients to help them with landing pages and lead magnets, it was a great success, and it was something that none of my competitors were offering – this is now something that is embedded into all of my programmes.

Using emerging technologies is also a good thing – remember when apps first came on the scene – imagine if we never adopted them into our businesses. And now there are all kinds of AI doing all kinds of things such as writing blog posts, social media content and even whole books – (No, I wrote this myself, but I did use ChatGPT for inspiration and editing purposes). They can also be utilised for creating images (I'll tell you how I do this in Part Four) analysing your data from Google analytics (simply genius) and all manner of other things. Look around and see what's available and how it can help you in your business.

One of the biggest advantages of being a small business is that you can adapt quickly. Large companies and organisations can take years to adapt to what is essentially a simple change. Use this advantage. Look for ways that you can beat the big businesses at their own game by being nimble and quick off the mark. Keep your ear to the ground about what those larger companies are focusing on right now and see if it is something you can do and do faster and easier (a good example may be trying to be carbon neutral).

Standing out among competitors is a constant challenge for small business owners. However, by implementing these five strategies, you can set yourself apart and carve a niche in the market. Develop a unique value proposition, build a strong brand identity, provide exceptional customer service, leverage digital marketing channels, and foster innovation. By combining these approaches, you'll establish a strong foundation for long-term success, capturing the attention and loyalty of customers while outshining your competition. Remember, being different and standing out is the key to thriving in a competitive marketplace and in the following chapters you will learn some simple techniques to help you do this effectively.

A great way to show you how standing out from crowd can make a huge difference to your business is to tell you a short story about a car salesman in America. Joseph Samuel Girardi, (better known as Joe Girard) was a car salesman in America between 1963 and 1978 and in that time he sold a whopping 13,001 cars – the most ever sold by one person ever! He appeared in the Guinness Book of Records for selling more cars than anyone else, and he won Top Vehicle Sales in The World award no less than 12 times - and in one year alone he sold 1425 cars – and all of them were retail, no fleet.

So, what made Joe so great at selling cars? Greeting cards. Yep, plain simple greeting cards. He would send out nearly 13,000 greeting cards a month to his customers celebrating everything from Groundhog Day to Halloween. Every year he would commission an artist to draw up 12 cards and then send them out. That's all he did. He would send out one card every month and each card had the same message "I like you". Receiving Joes cards on national holidays, birthdays, anniversaries etc the customers felt that Joe was part of the family and looked forward to receiving their monthly reminder of him.

It is probably prudent to point out that Joe employed two full time assistants to manage the card project and he paid them out of his own pocket from the enormous commission he made from his sales.

Joe Girard proved, without a doubt, that greeting cards inspire customer loyalty. Joe proved that greeting cards motivate customers to refer their friends. Of course, it was not the paper or colourful ink that did the trick, it was the man who cared enough to remember and honour his customers birthdays, anniversaries and holidays.

I think that story nicely demonstrates the impact that doing something different to what everyone else does can make a massive difference to your business and the outcome of your annual turnover. Today we have technology that makes this almost effortless – so why aren't we making more use of this wonderfully simple psychological trick and doing something similar for our customers?

Now that you know how important it is to Stand Out in your marketplace you are ready to move on to Chapter One where we will begin to put together your STAND OUT strategy, so stay tuned.

.

1 Your Vision and Mission

This chapter is going to help you come up with a definitive reason for why your business exists and what it's trying to achieve, and as part of that process we will be looking at your vision and mission statements. But you may well be wondering why creating a vision or mission statement is important for sales growth, because that is, after all, what this book is about, right?

Well, in the ever-evolving world of business, businesses need more than just goals and strategies to thrive. They require a compass that not only directs their actions but also gives them a sense of purpose and direction. This is where vision and mission statements come into play. Vision and mission statements are powerful tools that define the character of an organisation, providing a clear path forward and serving as a source of inspiration. A well thought out vision and mission statement can be used to inform many of your business decisions.

But before we dive into their importance to a business it is probably worth spending a moment or two to understand the distinction between the two. A vision statement outlines the desired future state or ultimate goal of a business, sharing its hopes and dreams and what it aims to achieve in the long term. On the other hand, a mission statement articulates the businesses' purpose, core values, characteristics, ethos and primary objectives, focusing on the present and the actions required to fulfil the vision. To make it easier to remember I thought of this little memory aid. Vision is for long term so long sighted (long-sighted being a condition to do with vision). Mission is for the present (I'm on a mission inferring it's happening now).

Vision and mission statements provide clarity and direction. They act as guiding principles that align the business, its employees and other stakeholders towards a common goal, making sure that everyone is working together towards the same end. By defining the purpose and values of the business, these statements can be used to create the framework for decision making, goal setting and resource allocation, leading to more focused and effective actions.

Vision and mission statements also inspire and motivate because they clearly outline the bigger purpose that the business is working towards. A well-crafted vision and mission statement can transform a group of individuals into a cohesive and effective team who are all working towards one clear outcome or objective.

As we've already mentioned in this part of the book, in a crowded and noisy marketplace businesses need to differentiate themselves in order to stand out and be noticed by their potential clients. Vision and mission statements play a crucial role in building a business's identity and establishing its unique position in the market. Done well, they can convey the values, beliefs and strengths that set it apart from its competitors. They can also play a part in attracting the right people to the business as it will be clear to a potential employee what the business stands for.

In today's dynamic and complex business environment, having a vision and mission statement is more critical than ever. These statements act as the foundation upon which successful businesses are built and can provide inspiration, clarity and a sense of purpose. By aligning stakeholders, guiding actions and establishing a unique identity, vision and mission statements can create a roadmap for success.

So now it's over to you. You need to think about what you want to say about your business. How are you going to align what you do with what you want to achieve? How are you going to ensure your stakeholders are aware of your vision and mission? How are you going to articulate your values and beliefs so that others recognise what you stand for?

Although this may seem like a daunting task it's really pretty simple when you break it down, and I am including a simple guide here to help you. At this point I would like to explain that The Business Builder, although owned and managed by myself and my son Chris, is made up of a team of other small business owners who support us in a variety of business building skills. We firmly believe in supporting as many as possible in whatever way we can and I must take a moment here to thank one of those small business owners for this simple framework that I have used myself and found to be extremely useful – thank you to the lovely Andrea Rainsford, SEO Angel.

Using the form below as a guide, first, enter your business name and strapline (the one sentence that sums up what you do) and your promotion channels (where people can find you both on and offline). This could be a local networking group, LinkedIn, Facebook group or website. Think of all the places your ideal customer could find you if they searched for you.

Vision & Mission

Business Name

Strapline

Promotion Channels

Why did you start your business?
(Give your top 3 reasons)

-
-
-

What are you most passionate about in your business?

-
-
-
-
-
-

What are your main ambitions for your business?

-
-
-
-
-
-

Now we are going to look at why you started your business. This is important because it will guide your decisions going forward. For example, I started my business because I wanted to help other small business owners to improve their online marketing so that they got better results and therefore made more sales more quickly. I had been clueless when I started out and so I knew from personal experience just how frustrating and upsetting it was when you did everything you could think of to attract new clients but no matter what you tried nothing seemed to work.

Next, we are going to look at what drives you in your business. What are you most passionate about and why. I was passionate about helping small business owners avoid the pitfalls and costly mistakes that I had made along the way. I was passionate about letting them into the secrets of the online marketing world so that they too could tap into its potential. I was also passionate about teaching, mentoring and supporting others and have been doing this in one form or another my whole working life.

Then we are going to look at your ambitions for your business. What is it that you really want to achieve? Where do you want your business to be in 3-, 5- or 10-years' time? My ambitions started off as small things like being able to replace my full-time income. I also wanted to help as many people as possible, although I didn't have a definitive figure in mind to begin with.

Look at the image below and complete these tasks. I would like to thank the wonderful Andrea Rainsford for providing the original idea and inspiration for the following worksheets.

Now we are going to look at the reasons for starting your business. It doesn't matter if you've been in business for a while, this exercise is still worth doing as it will take you back to basics and there have probably been a few changes since you started out. Look at the image below and answer the questions as honestly as you can. I have given some examples below if you need inspiration.

What is the **WHY** behind your business?

> What is your story?

> Why did you start your business?

> What is the main reason for wanting to run your own business?

> If you could do just ONE thing for the rest of your life, what would it be?

Write your answers below

_____

_____

_____

_____

_____

_____

_____

_____

_____

_____

I want you to think about your story – what was it that brought you to where you are today? For inspiration here's a little of my story…

… I was working flat out as a corporate trainer working for a large corporation and earning pretty good money. I had a large caseload but nothing I couldn't handle, or so I thought. One day, it was a Monday morning, I went for my usual morning swim and while I was swimming, I felt a stiffness in my neck. I didn't think too much of it at the time, but by Friday afternoon every single joint in my body had seized up. From the knuckles in my toes to my now almost immovable neck, every single joint was stiff. I could hardly walk, and when I did, I looked so ridiculous that my son nicknamed me Lego-legs, I'm sure you can picture why.

Obviously very concerned I made an appointment at the Doctors, and I got tested for everything from viruses to blood disorders and Rheumatoid Arthritis to Yellow Fever – nothing came back positive, which I guess was a good thing, but now I still had no idea what was wrong with me. This lasted for months and eventually the Doctor diagnosed it as a stress related disorder.

After considering my diagnosis I began to realise that I'd spent months working 12- and 14-hour days which had included a 90-minute commute each morning and then again at the end of the day. My weekends were usually spent catching up on stuff I hadn't had time to do in the office and the final straw came when a night out with friends that I'd been looking forward to having to be cancelled because I'd got too much work on to spare the time. It was time for a change. It was time to get my life back.

I looked around for something I could do from home and stumbled across a guy online who was talking about teaching people to sell anything to anyone anywhere in the world. It was called online marketing and apparently it was taking the internet by storm. I signed up for his free video course and then signed up for his amazing mentoring programme and over the next 3 years or so I learned a whole new skillset.

That wasn't so difficult, was it? Now let's look at WHY you started your business. Here's mine...

...After learning this amazing new skill and becoming an online marketer and selling all kinds of things to all kinds of people in all kinds of places I realised that other small business owners should know this stuff. I had been fortunate that I had come across this guy and that I was wealthy enough to be able to join his programme, but what about everyone else? I wanted to go out and teach other small business owners what I had learned so that they could improve their marketing and turn their businesses around. I wanted to make marketing simpler for everyone.

The main reason for wanting to run your own business is probably something personal to you – but you will know what it is so just write it down.

If you could do just one thing for the rest of your life, what would it be? This question is designed to get you thinking about what brings you joy. To be successful in business you must be passionate about what you do and be able to share that passion with others. So, think about all the things you do in your business and try to come up with something that you would happily do for ever more.

For me that's the training. I have been a trainer my whole career in one form or another and being able to develop other people's skills and knowledge and teach them how to implement those skills and that knowledge is what I am truly passionate about – hence being able to be talked in to writing this book.

Now we are going to try and formulate your vision for your business. Using the examples below try and complete your own Vision statement.

Examples

Choose clear and specific language. Dreaming big doesn't have to mean being vague, the perfect vision should be specific enough to influence your future business decisions.

You are not focusing on the past, add your dreams, ambitions, passions and goals. It is OK to dream BIG! No one got anywhere, dreaming small.

A vision could explain what your business would acheive if there were no barriers.

It's a description for your investors, partners, customers and employees - of where you could be in five, ten or even twenty years' time, and the impact you'd like your small business to have had on the world.

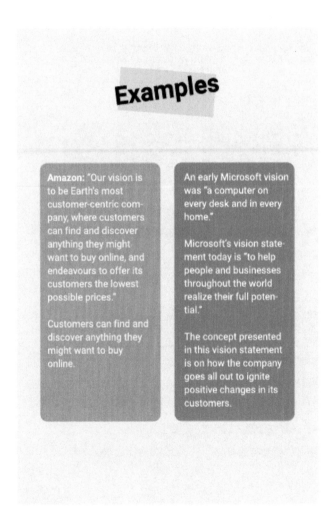

Examples

Amazon: "Our vision is to be Earth's most customer-centric company, where customers can find and discover anything they might want to buy online, and endeavours to offer its customers the lowest possible prices."

Customers can find and discover anything they might want to buy online.

An early Microsoft vision was "a computer on every desk and in every home."

Microsoft's vision statement today is "to help people and businesses throughout the world realize their full potential."

The concept presented in this vision statement is on how the company goes all out to ignite positive changes in its customers.

Okay, it's over to you. Using the examples above complete the following worksheet.

Think about what you want to say about your business. How are you going to align what you do with what you want to acheive?

Feasible: Is it a realistic and attainable vision?

Focused: Is it a clear vision to provide guidance in decision making?

Flexible: Does your vision allow alternative responses in light of changing conditions?

Communicable: Is it easy to communicate and be successfully explained in 5 minutes?

Now put it all together into one clear vision that you can use to inform your business decisions and that your customers will relate to.

Your **COMPLETE** vision

_____
_____
_____
_____
_____
_____
_____
_____
_____
_____
_____
_____
_____
_____
_____
_____
_____
_____
_____
_____
_____
_____
_____

My vision, as I mentioned earlier is Making Marketing Simpler for Everyone! My mission is helping small business owners improve their brand awareness and increase sales by supporting them with online marketing strategies. As you can see, they are simple, easy for my potential customer to understand and likely to resonate with them as I offer a solution to their problem which is not getting the results they want from their marketing efforts. Make sure your vision is somewhere you can see it every day, on your notice board, your screensaver or in your diary to review at least once a month.

2 Defining Your Goals

Fail to plan, plan to fail, an old saying but so pertinent to this chapter. Many businesses fail to plan and therefore fail to achieve their goals and objectives as they are constantly changing direction and being distracted by other things. Having a definite goal to work towards not only helps focus the mind of the business owner but also aligns the other stakeholders within the business so that everyone is working coherently as a team. Having clear goals will also help you stand out as a business as you will have a clear idea of your objectives towards your customers, how you intend meeting those objectives and everyone else involved in the business will know what those objectives are too. This clarity will be invaluable when it comes to creating your message (which we will get to later in Part One of this book) suffice to say that the clearer the message, the easier it is to attract your ideal customers.

Having a clear and well-defined set of goals is crucial for the success and longevity of any organisation. Goals serve as a guiding compass, providing direction and purpose to business, regardless of their size or industry. They act as a roadmap, outlining the best path to take in order to achieve desired outcomes and objectives.

Defining goals is not just a mere exercise; it is a strategic process that empowers businesses to align their efforts, allocate resources efficiently, and make informed decisions. By establishing goals, businesses create a sense of focus and clarity, enabling them to prioritise tasks, streamline operations, and maintain a forward momentum which will inevitably help with the overall success of the business.

One of the main benefits of setting clear goals is the ability to measure progress and track performance. Well-defined goals provide a benchmark against which businesses can assess their achievements and evaluate their growth. This allows businesses to identify areas of improvement, optimise strategies and make necessary adjustments to stay on track to reach their overall objectives.

Goals also provide motivation and inspiration to both leaders and employees within a business. When individuals have a clear understanding of what they are working towards, they become more engaged, committed and driven to succeed. Goals create a sense of purpose and a shared vision, fostering a cohesive and productive work environment where everyone is working as a team to achieve a common objective.

In addition, defining goals enables businesses to make informed decisions and allocate resources effectively. By understanding the desired outcomes, businesses can algin their investments, whether it be financial, human resource or technology, to support the achievement of those goals. This ultimately helps in avoiding wasteful expenditure and ensures that resources are channelled in the right direction which in turn maximises efficiency and profitability.

Goal setting can also provide businesses with the agility and adaptability needed to thrive. By regularly reviewing and reassessing goals businesses can respond proactively to emerging trends, shifts in the market and technological advances. This allows businesses to stay ahead of the curve, seize new opportunities as they present themselves and navigate challenges more effectively.

Now that you understand the importance of defining goals it's time to think of some goals of your own that will help your business achieve the outcomes and objectives it has set for itself. This chapter is going to help you define and create goals that you simply can't help but achieve.

Although you may think that is a bold claim, I can honestly say that if you follow the method laid out on the pages that follow you will be able to set goals confidently and effectively and know that they can be accomplished with ease.

There are many ways of describing goals in business: A big hairy audacious goal, a hairy scary goal, a stretch goal or they've even gone by the label "infinite purpose" but all of them have one thing in common, they are an effective and efficient way of achieving your business's desired results.

There are many frameworks available to you for creating goals, and you are free to do your own research if you choose, but I have never found anything better than the SMART goal framework for ease and understanding, until I came up with an upgrade to this framework which I will talk you through right now.

The acronym SMART stands for…
Specific
Measurable
Achievable
Realistic
Time-bound

We will go through each of these terms first, and then I'll show how I've improved the framework so that you cannot help but achieve any goal you set.

So, to begin with your goal needs to be **Specific.** Specificity is important here because we need to be crystal clear about what outcome you are aiming for. For example, it is no good just saying I want to increase my turnover. You need to know how much you want to increase it by, when you want to increase it by and how you intend to achieve it. Here is an example of a more specific goal...

I will increase my turnover by £100,000 in the next 12 months by introducing Google Ads into my marketing strategy.

Write down a goal that you would like to achieve in your business and be as specific as you can.

We then need to make sure that the goal is **measurable**. How will you know that you've achieved it? Of course, in our example that's just a case of a simple check with your accountant or looking at your numbers, but if your goal is more qualitative than quantitative you may need to be a little more imaginative about how you measure its success. A goal that can't be measured should be discarded as it will serve no purpose in the long term.

A goal must also be achievable. An achievable goal refers to a target or objective that can be reasonably accomplished within a specific timeframe, given the available skills, knowledge, capabilities and resources of the individual or business. It focuses on the feasibility and attainability of the goal, taking into account existing conditions and limitations.

In simple terms this means that you must examine the resources that you currently have. For example, do you need to gain a qualification, upskill, take on information or employ more staff in order to achieve this goal? If so, this may mean that it is not achievable in the timeframe you have set, and you may need to re-examine your goal.

If we look at our example above, we would need to consider the growth in terms of the financial amount (£100,000) and the timeframe we have set for ourself (12 months). If achieving our £100,000 involves selling more units we must be certain that we can increase those units without having to employ more staff, introduce new machinery or increase our warehousing capacity. However, if you can achieve £100,000 by simply taking on another 3 clients per month for a one-hour coaching session and you have spare capacity this would be very achievable.

Examine the goal you have written down. Is it achievable with the current resources available to you and in the timeframe you have set? If not re-write or reconsider your goal.

The next thing we must ask ourselves is whether the goal is realistic. A realistic goal considers not only the achievability but also the broader context and practicality of the goal. It will take into consideration such things as market conditions, industry trends and potential obstacles that may impact the goal's likelihood of success. A realistic goal acknowledges the need for flexibility and adaptation to overcome challenges and align with the overall strategic direction of the business.

If you're still unclear of the difference between an achievable goal and a realistic goal here is a simple way to think of it. An achievable goal concentrates on internal factors. A realistic goal concentrates on both internal and external factors. I hope that clears that up.

Examine the goal you have written down. Is it realistic in terms of today's current marketplace, industry trends or potential obstacles such as upcoming regulatory changes. If your goal is not realistic you may need to re-define it.

If we look again at our example above, we have stated that we will introduce Google ads into our marketing strategy as a way of driving extra sales to help achieve our goal of increasing our turnover by £100,000 in 12 months. We would need to do some research into things like cost per acquisition on Google compared to Bing or Facebook ads to make sure that we are getting the best return on our investment as Google is becoming more and more expensive as more businesses start up and use Google ads as a way of marketing their products and services to a wider audience.

Okay, now we come to the final letter of SMART – T. We need to make sure that our goal has a **time** limit. This is important because without a time limit, we will just flounder around and thus never achieve our goal, whereas giving it an end date will encourage us to keep the momentum going until the goal is achieved.

How long you give yourself to achieve your goal is entirely up to you, just so long as you keep within the achievable and realistic rules. Our example above shows that it can depend on what you are selling and how that is delivered. Businesses that are having to produce products will have more to consider than someone who works one-to-one with clients.

That is the SMART framework for creating great goals but I'm going to introduce a couple more letters which make those goals far more likely to be achieved. Those two letters are I and E so that we now have SMARTIE goals. Just by adding these two letters we are making our goals far more attractive and therefore far more likely to be realised. Why? Well stay tuned and I'll reveal all.

I is for **imagination**. Whilst studying for my psychology degree I learned that the brain cannot distinguish between what is real and what is imagined. A simple example of this by way of explanation is horror films. We KNOW that the person is NOT in our house – but we IMAGINE that we are in the house that is on our screen. Because the brain cannot distinguish the difference, when the intruder flashes in front of our eyes we automatically jump. We can use this to our advantage when we are setting our goals.

If we can imagine that we have already achieved our goal our brain will accept that as reality. This is important because if the brain thinks it's already happened it won't waste energy trying to talk you out of it. You will, no doubt, have experience of this phenomenon when you have tried to quit smoking, lose weight or take up a new skill or hobby. Your brain will have been trying to talk you out of it because it's something new and threatening and your brain is all about keeping the status-quo.

Let's go back to our goal above, here's a quick reminder of what it said…

I will increase my turnover by £100,000 in the next 12 months by introducing Google Ads into my marketing strategy.

Your brain will start saying things like "yeah, right. £100,000 – in 12 months, who are you trying to kid" or "that will mean you've got to take on more staff and that's more hassle you could do without" and on and on it jabbers until you finally acquiesce, and your goal is abandoned.

But if we imagine instead that the goal is already achieved and you already have that extra £100,000 in your accounts, your brain will accept that as reality and there will be no inner chatter trying to prevent you from smashing that goal. That is interesting, isn't it? And what's more, it absolutely works – but there's a catch.

Your imagination must be convincing. There can be no sign of doubt in your vision of the future. You must absolutely believe that you've achieved your goal. Now you may be saying that's all well and good but how do I convince myself of something that hasn't actually happened so convincingly that my brain doesn't see straight through the façade? That is a very good question, and I will endeavour to answer that now.

The answer is simple, you need to imagine how amazing it would be to have achieved your goal. How would you be feeling? What would you be doing differently? What would achieving your goal allow you to do that you can't do right now? The more detail you can give your vision the better because this is what will convince the brain that it has actually happened.

I recently worked with a client who set a goal to increase her business turnover from about £30K to £100K. I asked her to imagine what that would mean for her. She told me that she would love to be able to afford to move house. She wanted a house that was big enough for her to have her own workspace so that she could feel like a "proper" business. I asked her to imagine what this house would look like, what her office would look like, what colour scheme would she use, what decorations would she choose. I also asked her to imagine getting those 3 clients every month, where would they come from? How would she set up the initial meeting and what would she talk about.

Although she has not yet moved house, she has tripled her turnover so that's a great start as I'm sure you'll agree.

You might well be saying that you couldn't get very excited about increasing your turnover, or conjure up a convincing visualisation that would fool your brain, and I wouldn't blame you, so here's what to think about instead.

Why do you want to increase your turnover? Is it because you need to take on extra staff? Why do you need to take on extra staff? What will having those extra staff enable you to do? Why do you want to do that?

I was working with another client who wanted to earn an extra £3,000 in that year and during our goal setting session she said she was struggling to have a clear picture in her head of what that would look like. I asked her why she wanted to earn the extra money and she said so that she could do nice things for her daughters. I asked her what sort of nice things she wanted to do. She said that she wanted to take them to New York to visit family that they'd never met. I asked her if she could imagine being on the aeroplane, arriving in New York and being met by her sister and what they would do in New York as a family. She smiled and I could already see that picture forming in her mind. Sometimes you have to dig a little deeper to find your WHY. Once she realised that it was the OUTCOME and not necessarily the goal that she should be picturing it was much easier for her to visualise.

Did she do it? You bet she did, she had 3 wonderful weeks with her sister, cousins and extended family and her daughters were blown away by the whole experience.

Now that you have that perfect picture in your head it's important that you keep it there. Think about it every day. Make it the last thing you think about before you go to sleep at night and the first thing you think of when you wake up in the morning. Also think about it every time you feel a wobble coming on or someone tries to talk you out of it. The more you visualise the more real it will become for you so that it becomes a rock-solid certainty that it will manifest as reality and that in turn will encourage you to stick to your goal until the bitter end.

That brings us to the very last letter of this framework – E. E is for **emotion**. Attaching an emotion to a goal is vitally important as we are then more likely to be invested in its outcome.   Can you remember a time when you wanted something so badly that you would have done anything to get it. I remember wanting a leather jacket. They were trendy at the time and every one of my friends had one on their Christmas list. I badgered my mom day after day. I offered to do jobs around the house or the shopping or even the gardening if she'd just say yes to me having one.

Can you think back to that time? Can you remember the emotions that were tied up in that desire?   I remember imagining myself wearing the jacket, and as I imagined the scene my emotions took over. I felt good, fashionable and in with the in-crowd. That emotion of feeling so good about myself drove me to nag my mom half to death and offer to do pretty much anything I could think of – because I just had to have that jacket.

I'm pleased to say that my pestering paid off and I did indeed get that jacket. The minute I put it on I felt exactly as I had done in my imagination, and the emotions came bubbling up just as they had done a hundred times before when I'd imagined that moment.

I've used this same framework to gain a degree, lose weight, give up smoking, get my dream house, build my business and to get this book written. I have seen my clients achieve similar success when they apply the SMARTIE approach to goal setting, so it is my sincere hope that you put into practice what you have learned in this chapter so that you too can create goals you simply can't fail at.

In conclusion, defining goals is an essential aspect of strategic planning and business management. It empowers businesses with focus, direction and the ability to measure progress. By setting clear goals, businesses can enhance their performance, motivate their workforce, make informed decisions, allocate resources efficiently and adapt to an ever-evolving marketplace. In an era of intense competition and constant change, having well-defined goals is not just advantageous; it's imperative for long-term success and sustainability as they will help you stand out among your competitors.

3 What Are You Selling?

Matching what you sell to your customers' needs is crucial for the success and sustainability of any business and when you get this right it will elevate your position in your marketplace so that you stand out among your competitors and attract more of the potential market for that product or service. When you align your products or services with your customers' needs you create value and build strong relationships, which lead to several significant benefits:

1. Customer satisfaction. By offering products or services that meet your customers' needs you are enhancing their customer experience and therefore their satisfaction. When customers find that your products or services address their pain points, answer their questions or provide solutions to their problems they are more likely to be satisfied with their purchase and their experience of you as a business. Satisfied customers are more likely to become repeat customers

and cheerleaders for your business, driving positive and coveted word-of-mouth referrals.

2. Increased sales and revenue. When your offers align closely with your customers' needs, it leads to increased sales. Customers are far more likely to make a purchase when they can see the value and relevance in what you offer. By understanding their needs and preferences, you can tailor your offerings to meet their expectations and increase the likelihood of conversion. This, in turn, leads to higher business revenue and business growth.

3. Competitive Advantage. Matching your offerings to your customers' needs gives you a competitive edge. When your products or services address specific pain points or offer unique solutions to specific problems, you differentiate yourself from competitors. This differentiation allows you to position yourself as a preferred choice in the marketplace, attracting customers who are seeking precisely what you offer. By meeting your customers' needs better than your competitors, you gain a competitive advantage and strengthen your market position.

4. Customer Loyalty and Retention. When your offers consistently meet your customers' needs, it fosters customer loyalty. As we all know from personal experience, satisfied customers remain loyal to a brand or company and continue doing business with you over time. Building customer loyalty leads to higher retention rates and, according to research carried out by Avidly Agency, it has shown that it is 5X more expensive to find a new customer than to sell to an existing one. Loyal customers also have the potential to become brand ambassadors and cheerleaders for your business, promoting your business through positive reviews, recommendations and referrals. It's a well-established fact that 44% of companies have a greater focus on customers acquisition vs. 18% that

focus on retention, so by focusing on your current customers you will likely stand out from what your competitors are doing.

5. Long-Term Business Success. Aligning what you sell with what your customer wants is a fundamental element of long-term business success. It establishes a customer-centric approach that focuses on delivering value and building relationships. By consistently meeting your customer needs, adapting to changing market trends and continuously innovating your offers, you ensure your business remains relevant and competitive in the marketplace.

Think about what you are selling. Does it align with your customers' needs? Does it provide a specific solution to a specific problem? Let's look at a couple of real-world examples of how the big businesses do this to give context to this concept.

McDonalds offers fast food at low prices. Its customers are mainly lower to middle class consumers who are interested in fast, cheap and convenient food.

Mercedes Benz produce luxury cars. Its customers, throughout the brands history, are upper-class individuals above 40 years old who are interested in status.

Coca-Cola make fizzy drinks. Its main customer demographic is young people between the ages of 10 and 35.

Although the examples above are products, the same applies to providers of services. Let's take a look at one of my clients who came to me for help when she first started out as a life coach.

She was upset and frustrated because no matter what she did

she couldn't attract people who would pay for her services. The first question I asked her was who her ideal client was, and she began to real off a laundry list of who she could work with including men, women, children, those suffering a bereavement, those struggling with teenagers, new moms, divorced dads and pretty much the whole flippin' planet. No wonder you're struggling I said, you are trying to attract everyone so ending up attracting no one.

I explained that if she was going to be successful at attracting clients, she was going to have to align her offer to a particular group of people. Pick one, I said.

To begin with she argued and resisted saying things like, I can't get clients now and I'm advertising to everyone so how am I going to get clients if I cut my advertising down to just a few people? I told her the story of how I was introduced to this concept and what a difference it made to my business and has continued to do so ever since…

…Way back when I was learning online marketing and working with a coach, he told me I needed to find a product to sell online. He told me I could choose anything, so being a swimmer, I chose to sell swimming goggles. He told me to list my swimming goggles on Amazon taking care to list the benefits of my goggles compared to other, similar examples on the platform. It was difficult as there isn't much to choose between swimming goggles, so I did the usual listing that went something like this…

Swimming Goggles for Men/Women/Children. Available in Black or Silver. Adjustable strap for comfort. Anti-mist and UV protection for outdoors swimming.

I pressed the publish button and waited for my sales to come rolling in. To say I had a Luke-warm response is a bit of an understatement. I had one sale every few days and sometimes went a whole week with no sales at all. My coach then asked me to come up with ONE thing that set my goggles apart from all the other goggles on Amazon. I laughed and said I don't think there is anything different. He looked and me and said "Lynne, do you want to learn online marketing?" to which I obviously replied "yes, of course I do" he then said "well find that ONE thing that's different".

After a week or so of contemplating my goggles and turning them over and over in my hands I had come up with nothing. There was absolutely nothing different about my goggles than the goggles I had bought from Zogg or Speedo. Then, one day while I was rinsing my goggles in the shower, I noticed that the eye cups held a lot of water compared to my other goggles. That led me to think that they must have deeper eye cups than usual. I was overjoyed and couldn't wait to see my coach to tell him what I'd come up with. "great", he said, "Now who would that benefit?"

I thought about it for a long time and then it hit me like a slap in the face – "People with long or extended eyelashes" I proclaimed. "Great", he said "Now go and list them on Amazon as Goggles for people with long or extended eyelashes.

I was gobsmacked. What? I can't sell them as it is when ANYONE can buy them, so how can I hope to sell them if I'm just aiming them at the tiny amount of people who have long or extended eyelashes and are also swimmers? But as I was paying a lot of money for his advice, I figured I should follow it and I relisted my goggles on Amazon as this...

Best swimming goggles for long and extended eyelashes. Deep eye cups offer extra comfort. For men/women. Available in black/silver.

I sold more swimming goggles in the following week than I'd

sold in the two or more months before. My coach explained to me that the reason I was finally selling my goggles was that I was now aiming my goggles at a very specific group of people with a very specific problem (they wanted goggles that had deeper eye cups so that their lashes wouldn't rub on the inside of the eye cup). Because I was the ONLY person on Amazon selling swimming goggles for long or extended eyelashes, I was inevitably picking up all the sales from that group of people.

Now that my client understood what we were trying to achieve she agreed to go along with my method. She chose those struggling with teenagers as her ideal client as she was a parent of a troublesome teenager herself so thought that would be something she could talk confidently about in her marketing. We then put together an offer that said something along the lines of "Helping parents of teenagers to talk without the tantrums". Within 24 hours of putting out her post she had an enquiry. Within one month she had 3 clients and within one year she had niched down again and was now charging double what she had started out at.

The reason she became so successful is because she was talking to a specific group of people about specific problems, pain points and concerns. She was showing how she could help solve those problems quickly and easily and her message resonated with her intended clients.

Think about your product or service. How does it align with your intended clients' needs or expectations?

For a quick example of how this works for products think about your vacuum cleaner. A somewhat humble appliance these days, but how much more difficult would it be to clean your house without it? A customer who is looking to buy a vacuum cleaner is REALLY looking for something to help them get their housework done quicker and easier.

A coach needs to think about what transition their client is looking for. Where are they now in their lives and where are they trying to get to. Our example earlier where we were going to help parents of teenagers talk to them without the tantrums would meet them where they are at the moment, upset and frustrated that they can't communicate with their offspring and promises to take them to the point at which an adult conversation can be held. In this case our ideal client is REALLY looking for a way to effectively talk to their child.

Think about where your customer is today – what is it that they want? Write it down.

Now think about where your customer is trying to get to. Why are they struggling to get there on their own? Write it down.

Now think about your product or service. Is it the right thing for your customer now that you know more about them? If you need to make some tweaks or amendments now is the time to do it.

Failing to align your products and services with your client's needs can have detrimental consequences for your business. Without a clear understanding of your target audience and their specific requirements your products may fall short in meeting their expectations and fail to resonate with potential customers. It doesn't matter how great your marketing is, if your product doesn't resonate with your intended customer, you won't make sales.

Another thing you need to be aware of is the fact that most customers don't care how it's made, or where it's come from or how many modules there are or whether you have 26 letters after your name. The only thing most people are interested in is themselves. How is this product or service going to benefit me? What am I going to get out of it? Remember too that most customers are looking for a quick and easy fix. I was given an awesome piece of advice by one of my coaches many years ago, this is what he said…

Sell them what they want then give them what they need. To explain this a little better I will use one of my own marketing examples.

What my clients want is a quick and easy way to make more money. This is how I present my offer. I help you increase your turnover without having to increase your staff, your financial investment or your time in the office – and you can see results in as little as 4 weeks.

Once I've sold them what they want I can then set about giving them what they need, which is a proper marketing plan, a sales and retention strategy and a focused and detailed plan of action on how to scale once their target is met. But if I tried to sell that, people would take fright and disappear because it's too much and too overwhelming to consider.

Keep your product or service simple. Don't over-complicate it because it can do more harm than good. I have a personal example of how this backfired on a large car manufacturer. I was looking for a new car and quite liked the look of the Audi A1's. They were sporty hatchbacks and after borrowing one for a day I liked the drive, and it was nice and comfortable and had great road holding capability. I was convinced, I wanted one. I asked the car salesperson what I needed to do next and proceeded to tell me about all the different options that I could choose from. There were literally dozens, and I got confused and overwhelmed by all the choice. I finally made up my mind and told the salesperson what I had chosen. "Oh dear", he said "that option is only available in a 4 door". To cut a long story short I never did buy an Audi A1 – or any other Audi.

So, you see, I had too much choice, and in the end, I made NO choice. Take heed of my story and keep it simple for your customers. Don't give them a reason not to buy from you. Another one of my coaches told me this...

Sell one thing to one person at one price!

To be honest that was a bit hard for me to get my head around when I first started out in business as I wanted to offer different services at different prices and to different groups of people. The outcome was that I became overwhelmed with my marketing which led to it being non-specific and consequently I made few sales. Now that I'm a little more experienced I can see the value in this advice, and this is how I run my business today. I sell one product (my 4-week mentoring course) to one person (a business owner who needs help to increase their turnover) at one price (£3k). Does it mean I don't do anything else? No! I offer a business audit to identify growth opportunities for £500 and I offer a complete turn-key solution for those who want to build a business quickly (5K). The point is I use the 4-week programme as my chosen offer to get people to talk to me, once we are talking I can better tailor my offer to that particular person and their requirements.

4 Who Are You Selling It To?

Now that you've decided what you are going to sell it's time to figure out who you are going to sell it to. This is crucial for making sales easier as my swimming goggles example above demonstrated. You need to niche down as much as possible so that you can target a very specific group of people who have a very specific problem or desire.

I will just make a point here of letting you know that someone is 100 X more likely to buy something that solves a problem or alleviates a pain than they are to buy something that gives them pleasure. Attaining pleasure is seen as a luxury whereas eliminating pain is seen as necessity. If your product could do either I would focus on the pain and how it will help eliminate it.

To help you decide who your target audience is I've included my Bullseye Targeting Method as a visual aid which you can see in the image below.

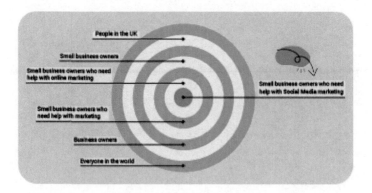

As you can see from the image, the rings represent a group of people and the smaller the ring the smaller that group is. For example, we begin at the outer, larger ring, and I have used this to represent everyone on Earth, all 8 billion of us, but as a business mentor I'm not looking to attract the whole planet, I'm looking for people who meet specific criteria.

The first criterion is that they speak English, as this is the only language I speak and thus trying to mentor someone who does not speak English would be far too difficult and not a very nice experience for the mentee, so I am going to target people in the UK. This has brought my potential audience down from 8 billion to around 60 million.

But I don't want to target everyone in the UK, I am only interested in those people who are business owners. I've narrowed my niche again by a few million. This is GOOD because it means I am getting more specific and targeted with my marketing and speaking to people about things they are interested in.

For the purposes of this exercise, I'm going to choose small businesses rather than medium or large businesses. It is important that I make the distinction because small business have different problems to those of larger businesses. For example, a large business may be worrying about its shareholders not getting their dividends or its marketing department's failure to communicate effectively with its sales team. A small business is probably far more concerned about no one engaging with them on Facebook – which is something I know I can help with. I've now narrowed my niche again by a few hundred thousand.

But I don't want to attract every small business. I'm only interested in attracting the attention of small businesses who are struggling with their marketing (another few thousand knocked off) and the only those who are looking for help with online marketing (another few thousand eliminated). I could have stopped there but here's the problem, there are many things involved in online marketing. For example, someone may need help with building a website, another may need help with creating email campaigns, someone else may need help with setting up a blog or a Shopify account. This would make it difficult to talk specifically to someone about one specific problem.

So, my bullseye target audience is small businesses who need help with social media marketing. This gives me a crystal-clear message to go out to my audience with. I can now talk about the things I know that audience will be interested in. I can put posts out about increasing followers, improving engagement, getting leads from LinkedIn or how to use the buy button on Instagram. I now have a clear message because I've got a clear idea of who I'm talking to.

But I don't stop there. Now that I have my group sorted, I want to think about who I most want to work with within that group. For example, I might only want to work with forward thinking, dynamic and energetic people. I might decide that I only want to work with people of integrity and who show compassion and understanding to others. Having a good idea of the type of person you want to attract will help you attract those people to you because you will talk in a way that appeals to them.

I recently put out a post that said I did not want to work with procrastinators on a workshop I was running because it was fast paced and we had no time for second guessing or periods of inaction. I did get one lady comment on my post and rule herself out as she said she was a procrastinator but under the right conditions she could be extremely productive and that I may be missing some good people by using language like that. She apparently missed my point entirely. I didn't want to work with people who couldn't keep up and I **wanted** her to rule herself out, as this speeds up the process of finding the right person for my programme.

I have included an image below of qualities which you might find useful. Try and pick three qualities that you would look for in an ideal customer. I like passionate action-takers who are punctual and respectful.

Qualities for Inspiration

Passionate	Open to change	Versatile
Action Taker	Humility	Adaptable
Tenacious	Loyalty	Curious
Diligent	Accountable	Individual
Organised	Resilient	Idealist
Ethical	Honest	Imaginative
Flexible	Respectful	Self-aware
Team Player	Compassionate	Wholehearted
Punctual	Integrity	Kind Hearted
Creative	Generous	Empathetic
Problem Solver	Dynamic	Intuitive
Drive	Energetic	Learner
Courage	Outgoing	Listener
Goal Orientated	Communicator	Persuasive
Knowledgeable	Perfectionist	Responsible
Optimistic	Humourous	Leader
Risk Taker	Respectful	Manager

You can also go one step further and come up with an avatar of your ideal customer, think of them as an actual person with a name, age, marital status, children, pets etc and then think about what it is that you can help them with. The more vivid your avatar the easier it will be to market to them.

The next thing we need to consider when defining our ideal client is where they are right now compared to where they want to be. This is important because if your product or service can get them to where they want to be quickly and easily you won't have too much difficulty in making sales.

Let's imagine a working woman with a family and 2 dogs. She is extremely busy but still wants her house to look nice and her family to look well presented. If this lady can afford it, she is most likely going to be open to a cleaner, an ironing service and possibly some sort of ready-made meal options that are nutritious and healthy. She will be attracted to these services because she wants a quick and easy solution to the problem of keeping on top of the household chores whilst also being a working woman.

But what if she can't afford to pay for someone to come and do it all for her? She still has the same problem, and she is still looking for the same solution "a quick and easy way of keeping on top of the household chores whilst also being a working woman". This lady would be more likely to look for the products that can make her life easier. For example, she would look for a slow cooker that she can set in the morning and have dinner ready when she comes home in the evening. She may prefer a steam generator to an iron as it can get the job done much quicker. She will be interested in static duster that lift dust with one quick swoosh across a surface and she will want the mop that dries the floor better after cleaning.

Our working woman is looking for ways to make her life at home as easy as possible but as we've seen above, her income may determine whether she is interested in a service or a product, and this is why you need to take the time to get to know your customer as well as possible and narrow your niche to those who would benefit most from your specific offer.

Imagine an accountant who is looking for new clients. Let's imagine the accountant is a man in this case. His first challenge will be to determine which kind of businesses he wants to represent. For example, he may want to work with tradespeople who are predominantly one-person outfits, or he may want to work with SME's with a turnover of up to £10M per year. Can you see how his marketing would be very different depending on which customer he is trying to attract?

A one-person outfit will probably need assistance with the bookkeeping element of accounting as well as the yearly (or quarterly tax returns). In contrast an SME will of that size will almost certainly have its own accounts department and possibly its own financial manager/director.

The language that the accountant would need to use would be very different in each example too. A small business owner wouldn't necessarily know what EBITDA (Earnings Before Income Tax, Depreciation and Amortisation) was, whereas a financial director would be fully conversant in this topic.

So, if our accountant were to take to social media or visit networking events to attract new clients, would he talk in a way that assumes that his client knows a thing or two about accounts and therefore confuses the sole-trader, or does he talk in a way that the sole-trader would understand and therefore put off the more knowledgeable businesspeople?

As you can see, not having someone specific to talk to means you are going to struggle to attract anyone.

The same is true of product-based businesses too. Imagine you are a jeweller. Do you want to attract the luxury/bespoke market, or do you want to appeal to the cheaper end of the market?

Again, you need to establish this BEFORE you go out to the marketplace as you will have completely different messages for each of the above. The high-end ticket will need to exude style, status and exclusivity whereas the low-end ticket will need to state value for money, versatility and attractiveness.

I hope that my examples have got you thinking about who it is that you are going to target with your products and services so that you can move on to the next chapter – Your Message.

5 Your Message

In today's fast-paced and interconnected world, where attention spans are shrinking and competition is fierce, effective communication has become paramount for businesses aiming to thrive in the market. Among the multitude of tools and strategies available, one aspect stands out as a crucial driver of success: messaging. Crafting the right message, tailored to resonate with the target audience, has the power to captivate, persuade, and ultimately influence consumer behaviour.

Messaging in marketing encompasses the art and science of conveying a brand's value proposition, core values, and unique selling points in a concise and compelling manner. It is the artistry of weaving words together strategically to evoke emotions, trigger curiosity, and establish a meaningful connection with potential customers. However, it also relies on the science of understanding consumer psychology, market trends, and the ever-evolving dynamics of buyer preferences.

This chapter delves into the significance of messaging as a cornerstone of marketing, exploring its essential role in capturing attention, building brand identity, and driving desired actions. Through a comprehensive examination of effective messaging techniques, we will uncover how businesses can leverage this powerful tool to differentiate themselves, amplify their reach, and create lasting impressions on their target audience.

Throughout this chapter, we will explore various aspects of messaging, including the importance of clear and concise language, the use of storytelling to engage and inspire, and the integration of messaging across different marketing channels. We will also delve into the significance of personalisation, emotional appeal, and the alignment of messaging with a brand's overall marketing strategy. By studying real-world examples and best practices, we will gain valuable insights into how successful companies have harnessed the potential of messaging to achieve their marketing objectives.

Whether you are a seasoned marketer looking to refine your messaging strategy or a business owner seeking to establish a strong brand presence, this chapter will provide you with the knowledge and tools necessary to create impactful messages that resonate with your target audience. By harnessing the power of messaging, you can effectively cut through the noise, capture attention, and leave a lasting impression in the minds of your customers.

The first thing to consider when creating your message is the language you use. In the previous chapter we talked about how an accountant can attract or deter potential clients by the language he uses and how using the right language can help "sell" your products or services because it resonates with the audience and creates an emotional bond.

One of the largest brands in the world had the message "Just do it".

Nike's "Just Do It" slogan has become synonymous with the brand and is an excellent example of succinct and motivational messaging. Introduced in 1988, this three-word phrase encapsulates Nike's commitment to pushing boundaries, overcoming obstacles, and embracing an active lifestyle. The simplicity and directness of the message resonate with athletes and fitness enthusiasts, encouraging them to pursue their goals fearlessly. By aligning the messaging with powerful visuals and inspiring stories, Nike has successfully built a strong emotional connection with its audience, making "Just Do It" an enduring and impactful marketing message.

Your message should reach your potential client on an emotional level. It should invoke feelings of achievement, that anything is possible and that by buying your product they can reach their goals and achieve their ambitions.

Another great example is "Belong anywhere", do you know who this slogan belongs to?

Airbnb's messaging revolves around the concept of belonging and the power of human connection. The "Belong Anywhere" campaign highlighted the idea that travelling is more than just finding a place to stay—it's about immersing oneself in local cultures and forging meaningful connections with people. This messaging tapped into the desire for authentic experiences and resonated with travellers seeking a more personal and immersive stay. By emphasising the emotional aspect of travel and the feeling of belonging, Airbnb's messaging successfully differentiated the brand from traditional accommodation options and created a loyal community of users.

These examples demonstrate the effectiveness of well-crafted messaging in marketing. By encapsulating the brand's values, evoking emotions, and connecting with the target audience on a deeper level, these companies have successfully created memorable campaigns that resonate and drive consumer engagement.

On a humbler scale, my message is "more wealth for everyone"

I want to convey a feeling of inclusivity, achievability and the acceptance that everyone can be wealthier. The use of the words "more wealth" are meant to conjure up visions within my audience of what they would have/do/be if they were wealthier. The word "everyone" is meant to convey that this is not just for those with a special skill, privileged background, private schooling or any other of those usual requirements to be able to access wealth.

If this is sounding a little familiar, good. It means you were paying attention when we did the Vision and Mission activity in Chapter One. But now we are going to take that message and build on it a little so that it becomes an offer that your customer will want to take you up on.

You will now spend some time crafting your message so please follow the guidelines below…

Your message needs to stand out and be clearly understood by your potential customers.

Your message needs to be consistent so that you are not confusing your audience.

Using this format can help you create messaging that is crystal clear and consistent.

On a piece of paper or your laptop list all the benefits of your product or service (benefits, not features) Here's the difference if you're not sure

Feature = High-definition camera
Benefit = Create beautiful memories in an instant

Feature = 6-week programme
Benefit = Quickly become more confident so that you are able to say no when you need to.

Feature = Programmable memory
Benefit = Never forget anything again

Feature = Hand crafted
Benefit = Enjoy one-of-a-kind products that are as induvial as you.

Now list all the benefits of your product or service.

Now think about who that product or service could help – Remember my swimming goggles? They helped people with long or extended eye lashes. Use your piece of paper or laptop to list out the customer niche you think is a good fit for your product/service.

From the list of potential customers that you created from the exercise above please now choose one and write it down.

Now come up with a message that is a similar format to this one…

"Helping you increase your turnover without increasing your staff, financial investment or time in the office – and in just 4 weeks"

Think of the verb you want to use, here are some to consider:

Helping, supporting, creating, empowering, manufacturing, providing, assisting, managing

Now add what your product or service does eg. Creating bespoke Jewellery

Now add the ideal customer you chose earlier eg.

Creating bespoke Jewellery for discerning ladies

Now add one of the benefits you came up with earlier eg

Creating bespoke Jewellery for discerning ladies who want to look and feel special

You now have a message that you can use that is clear.

It says what your product is, who it's for and why it's special.

Of course, over time you will come up with better messaging, but this will be a great start and will make sure that you attract the right people from the outset.

If it's appropriate to do so you can use the sentence you just came up with as your headline or bio in your social media – or at least use it somewhere in your profile on LinkedIn and grid on Instagram.

Over time you will collect ideas from other people who you see marketing similar products or services to you, and you should keep a note of the ones that drew your attention so that you can come up with something similar for your own messaging.

Story telling is also a great way to get your message across. Human beings have been telling stories since the beginning of time – cave paintings used to tell the stories of what people hunted and how they lived. We have never tired of stories and they have continued to be told throughout the ages from William Shakespeare to Charles Dickens and on to the big blockbusters on our screens today.

Telling your story is an important part of standing out as it shows you as an individual, unlike anyone else, with your own unique way of looking at things and your own personal experience of life. This uniqueness is what will make you stand out among everyone else. Telling your story will help your potential clients get to know you – the person behind the business.

There's no need to tell all your deepest, darkest secrets, just share your business journey, your why, your hopes and dreams, your challenges and how you overcame them. People love learning about people – we always have.

I have found that when I tell stories on my social media I get far more engagement and reach than from anything else I post. My audience gets to know me a little more and they can relate to me a little more which means I am more approachable than someone who only ever posts about business.

You can also tell stories about the people your products or services have helped. What outcome did you get for them, how did they respond, what are they doing now that they couldn't do before. These are called case studies and offer a powerful way of getting your message across as it will be talking about people who are just like your intended customers achieving the results that your intended customers want to achieve.

There are many types of story that you can choose from: rags to riches, journey, origin or superhero. I will briefly cover what each one is so that you can choose which one(s) fits you best.

Rags to riches is a story to use if you help people make money. Using your own story of how you struggled to (whatever your customer is struggling with) and how you then discovered (what you are now sharing with your clients) and how it changed your life and what you are doing now that you couldn't do before.

Journey stories are great as they show how a business got started and why it started. Fairfax and Favor are a great example of how they use an origin story to engage with their audience and I'll share it in a moment so that you can see how impactful it is.

Origin stories are about where you came from. What got you started on your business journey and why. What were you hoping to achieve and who were you hoping to help and why is that so important.

Superhero stories are stories that show the impact you/your products/your services have had on others. How have you changed lives, how have you stopped something from happening, started something, cured something etc.

I have found that the best stories are the ones that come from the heart. The ones that have you tearing up as you write them, or wandering down memory lane and smiling at the words as they appear on the screen.

It is also worth remembering that story telling is not just for your social media. You can tell stories in your blog, on your website, in your networking meetings and on other people's stages. In fact, the more places you find to tell your stories the more people will get to hear them, and the more customers you will acquire.

We have also touched a little on the significance of emotional appeal and I would like to cover this a little bit more here as it is an important factor in the success of your message.

Being able to tap into someone's emotions has always been known to be the most effective marketing strategy. Now don't misunderstand me, I don't mean manipulation or taking advantage of someone's vulnerabilities as that would be unethical and is certainly not something I advocate or teach my clients to do.

Earlier we talked about a working woman with a busy household to look after and her desire for a quick and easy way to keep her house and family clean and well presented. I want you to think about what emotions are surfacing when that woman thinks about cleaning her house.

Perhaps she has feeling of dread, or exhaustion, or resentment, or perhaps she doesn't mind the cleaning but just wishes it didn't take up so much of her day. Perhaps she would much rather have taken her son to his swimming lesson that morning rather than having to send him off with a friend.

Knowing what emotions are present when she thinks about cleaning means that our cleaning company can come up with messaging that speaks directly to her so that the message resonates and is therefore far more likely to lead to an action.

For example, let's imagine that our cleaning company have a message something like this...

Stop missing out on your kids growing up. Let us do the chores so that you can enjoy the parenting.

There is a tool I use with my clients for helping them figure out more emotive messaging. It's a free tool (or at least it was at the time of writing this book) and it's called A.M Institute Headline Analyser. Go and check it out, it will help you come up with phrases that will hook your audience on an emotional level so that you stand out and attract more customers for your goods and services.

I'm fairly certain that this message would stop our lady in her tracks when she saw it, as it is exactly what she is thinking, and it invokes that emotion of missing out on her son's swimming lessons.

Personalisation is also something to consider when crafting your message. Remember, the more specific it is to a particular person the more inclined they will be to remember it and act on it. Again, remember my goggles for people with long or extended eyelashes? This was a product aimed at a very particular group of people that spoke directly to them.

I hope that as you have read through the pages of this chapter you have realised that getting your messaging right is the best thing you can do in terms of marketing your products or services. A good message will stand out for its intended audience, connect with them on a personal and emotional level and inspire and encourage them to take action.

Spending time on your message is time well spent and will pay dividends. Make sure you get to know your intended customer well. Think about the emotions they are experiencing and how your product or service can take advantage of this. Think about the benefits that your product or service offer and try to incorporate them into your message.

"Think Different"

Apple's iconic "Think Different" campaign, launched in 1997, remains a classic example of powerful messaging. The campaign celebrated the spirit of innovation and individuality by featuring influential figures like Albert Einstein, Martin Luther King Jr., and Mahatma Gandhi, among others. The simple yet thought-provoking message conveyed Apple's commitment to challenging the status quo, inspiring creativity, and appealing to those who dared to think differently. This messaging not only reflected Apple's brand identity but also resonated deeply with its target audience, positioning the company as a leader in innovative technology.

And, if you're wondering just how much of a leader they were consider this, without the Apple iPhone there would be no Apps! Can you imagine a world without Apps now?

Here's a quick reminder of those steps...

Think of the verb you want to use, here are some to consider:

Helping, supporting, creating, empowering, manufacturing, providing, assisting, managing

Now add what your product or service does eg. Creating bespoke Jewellery

Now add the ideal customer you chose earlier eg.

Creating **bespoke Jewellery for discerning ladies**

Now add one of the benefits you came up with earlier eg

Creating **bespoke Jewellery for discerning ladies** who want to look and feel special

Now go and create messaging to inspire your audience.

6 The WOW Factor

In today's highly competitive business landscape, small businesses face numerous challenges when it comes to standing out from the crowd. One powerful tool that can help them leave a lasting impression on customers and differentiate themselves is the "wow factor." This chapter explores why the wow factor is crucial for small businesses and how it can contribute to their success as well as exploring ideas that you can adopt into your own business.

Although there are many advantages to having a wow factor in your business, I am using the five examples below to illustrate how it can help to grow your business by helping it stand out and therefore attract new customers quickly and retain old customers more easily.

1. Captivating Customer Attention: In an era of information overload, capturing the attention of potential customers is more challenging than ever. The wow factor acts as a magnet, drawing people's

attention to a small business and piquing their curiosity. By incorporating unique and memorable elements into their products, services, or overall customer experience, small businesses can effectively engage customers, creating a strong initial impact that encourages further exploration.

2. Creating Memorable Experiences: Small businesses have the advantage of being able to offer personalised experiences that are often absent in larger corporations. Implementing the wow factor allows them to create moments that customers remember long after their interaction with the business. Whether it's through exceptional customer service, innovative products, or unexpected surprises, these memorable experiences foster positive word-of-mouth and repeat business.

3. Differentiation and Competitive Edge: Small businesses often find themselves competing with larger, more established companies with greater resources. The wow factor provides a means for small businesses to differentiate themselves from their competitors, effectively carving out their own niche in the market. By offering something unique, remarkable, or highly desirable, small businesses can attract customers who are seeking alternatives to mainstream options.

4. Building Brand Reputation and Loyalty: The wow factor plays a pivotal role in shaping a small business's brand reputation and fostering customer loyalty. When a small business consistently delivers on its promises and goes the extra mile to surprise and delight customers, it builds a reputation for excellence and innovation. Such positive associations strengthen

customer trust, which in turn leads to increased loyalty and advocacy. Satisfied customers are more likely to become brand ambassadors, sharing their positive experiences with others and contributing to organic growth.

5. Amplifying Marketing and Publicity Efforts: In today's digital age, the wow factor can significantly amplify a small business's marketing and publicity efforts. When customers are genuinely impressed by a product or service, they become willing advocates, sharing their experiences on social media platforms, review websites, and through word-of-mouth. These organic endorsements can generate substantial exposure and attract new customers, often at a fraction of the cost of traditional advertising methods.

Think about the last time you said wow! How were you feeling at that time? I would suggest elated, excited, pleased, pleasantly surprised or some other equally good feeling.

When a customer says wow, it means you have gone above and beyond, you have exceeded their expectations in some way, and they will experience one of those good feelings we mentioned above which in turn will mean they are feeling good about your business.

Having ways to wow your customers should be part of your marketing strategy as being able to delight and surprise them will make it easier to forge long-lasting relationships and connections which will lead to more clients and increased turnover.

Wowing your customer doesn't have to include some grand and expensive gesture, it can be the simplest little thing that can make all the difference, and you can begin wowing them before they become a customer.

For example, I arrange one-to-one meetings with people I network with to get to know them a little better on a personal level. I turn up with a small gift for them. These little gifts cost just a few pennies but the look on their faces when they receive them is priceless – they won't forget our one-to-one in a hurry.

Another example of how I wow my customers BEFORE they are customers is to offer something of immense value – for FREE! I record short video tutorials that explain how to do something that I know they are struggling with, and I offer these for free on social media as a "lead magnet". A lead magnet is something that is offered in exchange for someone's email address, but we will cover this in more detail in Part Two of this book.

A recent example of one of my lead magnets is "How to Become a Standout Person In Your Profession". I offer a free video tutorial that gives my audience hints and tips to help them rise above the crowd so that their potential customers see them, hear them and remember them.

I know my audience is struggling to find customers, so I am offering to solve this problem for them by teaching them how to generate more leads by standing out from their competitors, something that my audience would think of as valuable information.

The information in my tutorial is actionable and easy to do, and, if applied, will bring results. Imagine having your problem solved in one simple solution and for free, how pleased and surprised would you be? Would you say Wow, I can't believe I got that much information for free?

Of course, this method is, like most of my other methods, based in psychology. I want my clients to be impressed, to learn to trust me and be confident that what I teach works. I also want them to think that if I give that much away for free, how much more do I give when they pay for it. I am building what we call in the marketing world, the know/like/trust factor. People buy from people, but they mostly buy from the people they know, like and trust.

Businesses will have many "touch points" where they interact with their potential customers and thus an opportunity to surprise and delight them before they make their first purchase, but most businesses do not take advantage of this opportunity. Most businesses only think about wowing their customers once they have become a customer.

Think about how you can introduce the Wow factor to your potential customers.

What could you offer as a free download that your customer would find helpful, useful, informative, inspirational or valuable? Write your ideas down so that you can sift through them later. Below are some ideas that might help you decide what you could do.

Checklist

"How-to" guide	Flip Book
E-book	Online Course
Brochure	Discovery Call
Spreadsheet	Blueprint
Money off voucher	Cheat Sheet
Free Trial	Swipe File
Video Tutorial	Challenge
Email Course	Bootcamp
Templates	Masterclass
Printables	Workshop
Book	Free Demo
Discount Code	
Webinar	

If you meet people in person there are other things that you can give away that will surprise and delight them. Remember my little trinkets, they didn't cost very much but they were a great way for me to stand out and be remembered when that potential client is deciding who to buy from at a later date.

Touch points are the times and places where you meet your potential customer. This may be on your social media or website, in a networking meeting, in a one-to-one meeting or during a discovery call. What will you do to wow that person at every point of contact?

Here's an example of what I do…

On my social media channels I offer lead magnets that I know will help them solve a problem or alleviate a pain point.

On my website I have a free resources for them to access and learn from.

In my emails I offer further help, advice, hints and tips to help them grow their businesses.

At my initial one-to-one in-person meeting I take a gift. If it's an online one-to-one I offer them a free blueprint call.

On the free blueprint call I create a growth plan that helps them take advantage of every opportunity so that they can increase their turnover without having to increase their workload. They get this growth plan to take away and start putting in place that very same day.

When they sign up to my S.E.L.L. System programme I send a parcel to their home address with a nicely designed, branded and professionally printed set of workbooks, a notebook for them to keep all their notes together in one handy place, a small gift such as a badge or pen, a card that tells them to remember how awesome they are and a welcome letter that tells them all about what they will be doing as part of the programme.

During the programme I continue to wow them with content that goes above and beyond what they expected, and support with things they didn't even know I knew about, in fact, one of my clients recently said "Wow, Lynne, you're a thousand different things all rolled into one aren't you."

After they have completed the programme, I continue to wow them with emails that give them further information and support – for free. I also offer them an affiliate programme where they get paid for introducing me to new clients.

As you can see from my example above, I have 8 touch points where I can take the opportunity to wow my clients. How many touch points do you have in your business and what can you do at each touch point to wow your customers?

In conclusion, the wow factor holds immense importance for small businesses as it helps them cut through the noise, create memorable experiences, differentiate themselves from competitors, build brand reputation and loyalty, and amplify their marketing efforts. By consistently delivering unique and exceptional experiences, small businesses can foster customer engagement, retention, and growth. Embracing the wow factor allows them to create a lasting impact on customers and thrive in a competitive business landscape by helping them stand out from the crowd.

Part Two: Engage

Introduction: Captivating Hearts and Minds - The Power of Engaging Your Audience

In a world overflowing with information and distractions, capturing the attention and interest of an audience has become an art form. Whether you are a public speaker, a writer, a marketer, or a business owner, the ability to engage your audience is a skill that can set you apart from the crowd and lead to remarkable success. Part Two of this book delves into the profound importance of audience engagement and offers valuable insights, strategies, and techniques to master this captivating art.

Chapter by chapter, we will explore the transformative effects of engaging an audience across various domains. We will uncover the secrets behind captivating headlines that move hearts, compelling stories that resonate with readers, marketing campaigns that create a buzz, and business strategies that forge long-lasting connections. Through real-life examples and practical exercises, you will embark on a journey to unlock your own potential as a masterful engager.

Engaging your audience is more than simply grabbing their attention; it is about forging a genuine and meaningful connection that compels them to listen, participate, and take action. It is about wowing and wooing them and creating an experience that lingers in their minds long after the interaction is over. By understanding the psychology of engagement and harnessing the power of emotions, you can elevate your communication skills to new heights and leave a lasting impact on those you seek to inspire.

In this part of the book, we will delve into the core principles of audience engagement, including:

1. The Art of Storytelling: Discover the persuasive power of storytelling and learn how to craft narratives that captivate, inspire, and evoke emotions. Explore the essential elements of a compelling story and uncover storytelling techniques that will enable you to connect deeply with your audience.

2. The Psychology of Engagement: Dive into the minds of your audience and unravel the psychological triggers that stimulate interest, curiosity, and active participation. Understand how to tap into their desires, values, and aspirations, and learn how to tailor your message to resonate with their needs.

3. Building Authentic Connections: Explore the significance of authenticity in building trust and

establishing genuine connections with your audience. Discover how to be relatable, empathetic, and transparent, creating an environment that encourages open dialogue and active engagement.

4.   The Power of Visuals and Multimedia: Embrace the influence of visual communication and multimedia in capturing attention and enhancing engagement. Learn how to incorporate captivating visuals, videos, and interactive elements to enhance your message and create a multisensory experience.

5.   Interaction and Feedback: Recognise the importance of two-way communication and the value of incorporating audience interaction and feedback. Explore various techniques to encourage participation, foster dialogue, and create a sense of ownership among your audience.

Throughout the following chapters, I will equip you with the tools, strategies, and inspiration to take your audience engagement to new heights. By mastering the art of captivating hearts and minds, you will elevate your personal and professional endeavours, leaving a lasting impact on those who have the privilege of experiencing your message. Get ready to embark on a transformative journey that will empower you to engage, inspire, and create a meaningful connection with your audience.

7 Storytelling

Storytelling has emerged as a powerful marketing strategy because it taps into the fundamental human desire for narratives and connection. It goes beyond merely selling products or services by engaging customers on an emotional level and creating a lasting impression. Here are some reasons why storytelling is so effective as a marketing strategy:

1. Emotional Connection: Stories have the ability to evoke emotions and connect with people on a deeper level. Emotionally charged narratives capture attention, resonate with personal experiences, and create a sense of empathy. By triggering emotions such as joy, nostalgia, or inspiration, storytelling can forge a strong bond

between a brand and its audience, making the marketing message more memorable and impactful.

2. Engaging and Memorable: Stories are inherently engaging and memorable. They have a natural flow that captures attention and sustains interest. When information is presented in the form of a story, it becomes more relatable, easier to understand, and more likely to be retained. This makes storytelling an effective way to communicate complex ideas, brand messages, or product benefits, as customers are more likely to remember the information embedded within a narrative structure.

3. Differentiation and Brand Identity: In today's crowded marketplace, it's crucial for businesses to differentiate themselves. Storytelling offers a unique opportunity to showcase the values, mission, and personality of a brand. By crafting a compelling brand story, businesses can stand out from competitors and create a distinctive identity that resonates with their target audience. This helps to build brand loyalty and attract customers who align with the brand's values and narrative.

4. Building Trust and Authenticity: Trust is a vital factor in establishing customer relationships. Stories have the power to humanise a brand, making it relatable, authentic, and trustworthy. When businesses share their origin stories, customer success stories, or narratives that

highlight their commitment to social responsibility, they create a sense of transparency and build trust with their audience. By showcasing the real people and values behind the brand, storytelling helps to establish credibility and foster long-term customer loyalty.

5. Memorable Brand Recall: People are more likely to remember stories than dry facts or data. When a brand incorporates storytelling into its marketing strategy, it creates a memorable experience that lingers in the minds of customers. As a result, customers are more likely to recall the brand and its message when making purchasing decisions. Storytelling helps to embed the brand in the customer's memory, increasing the chances of brand recognition and preference in the future.

6. Viral Potential: Stories have the potential to go viral and reach a wide audience. When a story resonates with people, they are inclined to share it with others, leading to organic word-of-mouth marketing. Compelling narratives have the power to create a buzz, generate social media discussions, and attract attention from media outlets. This viral potential amplifies the reach of a brand's message and increases its visibility, often at a fraction of the cost of traditional advertising.

To put all of this into context I thought it might be a good idea to share an example. This is Fairfax and Favor's origin story from its website, one of my personal favourites…

"Behind every brand is an untold story and ours is no different... except to say our story is a little different. Late in the spring of 2012, our yet-to-be founders, Marcus & Felix, made an ambitious pact: to combine their middle names and launch their very own footwear brand; one that would specialise in luxury boots and shoes inspired by country life. They wanted to pioneer rural vogue accessories and, despite having no idea how, nothing was going to stop them. Fairfax & Favor   was   their   future.

Fast forward a few weeks later, while they were thinking long and hard about their next step, Felix was hit by a lightbulb moment: his godfather sold leather gun slips manufactured in Spain, a country celebrated for producing some of the most beautiful leather shoes in the world. That was their in... to the world of leather at least.

They were right. Spain was promising. But establishing which country to start their treasure hunt for the finest shoemakers was only one problem solved. There was still the matter of actually finding a factory that would help them and then being able to pay that factory for their help. But having had zero luck with the former, they decided to focus on funds and how exactly they would bootstrap their new venture of handcrafted leather   footwear.

The answer; use their University's excessively long summer break to work hard and spend very little. It worked. They split their time between pub shifts at The Bedingfeld Arms and working as a fireplace delivery team for After The Antique, before combining their summer savings with their young-blood desire to prove boots could be made well - the way they ought to be - and still look great in both the city and country.

Next up was acquiring their first batch of shoes and boots, namely where to make them and how.

We found a factory in Spain that made shoes. That was the good news. The bad news was, we had to order 420 pairs. It was the same everywhere. The money we had saved was not enough. It wasn't even close. With nothing to lose, we found some cheap flights to Alicante, landed in Spain, jumped on a bus and walked around some town at the foot of some mountains   for   hours   and   hours.

With our funds dwindling fast, we scrabbled together what little Spanish we knew and asked the receptionist at a local school for directions. She went one better; for 50 euros, she offered to call the factory on our behalf and schedule a pick up. We agreed, and the next day four trucks rode into the centre of town, picked us up and then left Dodge in a cloud of smoke. We climbed mile after mile into the mountains, each hairpin bend shaking our nerves, turning any excitement we had felt into brilliant regret, we had been kidnapped.

Of course, they quashed this hasty conclusion of ours by showing us around their factory. The factory agreed to make 420 pairs of off-the-shelf loafers and deliver them within four weeks, but one condition: we paid every cent upfront. We agreed, shook hands, flew home via a few sangrias and spent what felt like an eternity pulling pints and delivering fireplaces, the thought of "what have we done?" hanging heavy on our minds.

Six weeks later, 390 pairs of Fairfax & Favor branded shoes arrived on our doorstep. It wasn't quite what we had agreed but, for some reason, we didn't feel like complaining. Our first rookie mistake was storing the 390 boxes of shoes in mum's attic. Logistically, it was horrendous, while sweeping it clean of dust can only be described as "medically inadvisable". Still, we had our shoes, we had them stored somewhere safe, and we had a plan; doorstep a bunch of shops in Norwich and have them buy our shoes... well, easier said than done.

One shop bought £80 worth of shoes, another agreed to take ten pairs and pay on sale, while another took some of our stock but, now we think of it, never actually paid. It was a heroic death. But we did learn something from this failure; the fastest way we could generate cash was to coerce our friends and family into buying the shoes.

If we ever wanted to clear the 300-plus pairs of shoes that were still playing clutter in the attic, we only had one option; sell direct. Cue our first show season.

In the summer of '13 with next-to-nothing in the bank, no friends left and a few unpaid bills on the to-do list, we approached Holkham about getting a pitch at their Country Fair, trying our luck two days before it kicked off. Luckily, someone had just pulled out. There was a patch of grass available, six meters by four. Unfortunately, it came with a £600 price tag.

Embracing the spirit of Alicante, we drove to the Holkham offices, charmed them down to £200 (OK, and a pair of shoes each for the office staff) and went about setting up our first ever stand, which was assembled out of an old gazebo, our living room sofa, bar tables from the pub, old cabinets, tuck boxes, trunks and anything else that looked a bit like treasure if we squinted hard enough. The only thing we spent money on was the Fairfax & Favor sign. It was £25. And we propped it up with two shooting sticks found in an old stable. It was rough,   but   it   was   home.

With the sun shining down on us like a new penny, we sold 80 pairs of shoes. It was enough to cover our costs and pay for a pitch at the next one. It was the start of our love affair with shows and, in an attempt to keep the momentum going, we vowed to invest everything we made back into the company. No exceptions.

After a year of growing Fairfax & Favor by day, manning the pub by night and delivering fireplaces on any weekend we had off, things started to improve. We began paying ourselves a small token wage a week and focusing every minute we had on shoes. No more pub or near-death experiences attempting to deliver   1/2   tonne   slabs   of   stone.

We converted an underground loo into our office and started using an old stable as our storeroom. The days of lugging hundreds of boxes up and down the attic-ladder after each show   were   now   behind   us.

Of course, it wasn't all roses and sloe gin because getting the stable storeroom-ready was atrocious. It was a century-old scrapyard of junk, dust, festering manure and asbestos. Oddly enough, we don't have a picture of this day on our wall.

While choosing designs in Alicante, we had naively chosen an off-the-shelf loafer that had a snaffle buckle. It was a gorgeous design and we were little more than dreamers, not experts in copyright infringement. It didn't matter. We received a 92-page letter from a famous Italian brand threatening to sue us. To say it made us quake in our inspired loafers would be an understatement. But there was more. The letter arrived at 5.30pm on a Friday, which was real weekend-ruiner and the first few pages of the letter constituted a list of law suits they had won. It wasn't the most uplifting bedtime read. The future of Fairfax & Favor was heading for a cliff edge, our name set to take a nosedive and land with a splat at the bottom of their list, no doubt filed under "Squashed Dreams".

Their demands were staggering. A £100,000 fine, a full-page apology in the telegraph, receipt of all our shoes and our signature on a document that stated we would never be so foolish to mess with the brand again. It was terrifying. They were threatening to sue us, they had lawyers that dealt with Diana's divorce from Charles. They had lawyers you call when you want to divorce a future King and we had Mark from Swaffham; the cheapest lawyer money could buy.

Mark's plan? To get the £100k fine reduced to £40k. The problem? This was still more than twice our annual turnover. Luckily, we managed to convince another lawyer to send an email on our behalf. We won't go into details, but he used the phrase "I would like to educate you on a point of law" and then offered them a deal to pay much-much-much less, send back all the shoes and sign their document. They Agreed. Thank God. And thank God they had sent that letter on the Friday because we were about to order another 800 pairs.

Sending the shoes back hurt but, being young and foolish, we had some fun. We mixed all the shoes, sizes and colours so that no box contained a matching pair. Yes, the famous Italian brand had the last laugh, but we enjoyed a little snigger before the curtain fell.

There is a moment in everyone's life when the game changes – when all the daydreaming, night-thinking, blood, sweat, tears and hopes of what if finally come together. For us, that moment arrived when we gave the Spanish bota a different song   to   sing.

We saw something that no one else had and so we set about transforming this once clunky workhorse into a glass slipper now known as the "Regina" boot. With its slim-fit, stylish heel and an interchangeable tassel, we had turned this farmhouse plodder into a polished piece fit for the runway.

Regina has been our lucky charm ever since.

Year-on-year at the tail end of July, our entire team gear up in preparation for a full-blown magical weekend of boots, shoes, sunshine and showers as we fly our flags high for the Game Fair.

To us, the Game Fair is more than just a show. It is a milestone, one that overcomes us with a monumental sense of pride and achievement. In our early days, the show circuit was a daunting prospect; we were miniscule fish in a monstrously large pond, and didn't we know it. We paddled in the shallow end for a few years, with a 3 metre stand here and a 6 metre stand there, but it was in 2015 where the Game Fair allowed us to really push the boat out, giving us our first real opportunity for our first BIG pitch and oh boy, were we going to make the most   of   it.

A bigger pitch meant more space, a whole 9 metres to be precise. 9 metres meant more customers, more customers inevitably equated to more sales, more sales required more stock. It was turning into a military operation, one which required us to collar all of our closest friends to help muck in with no objection; we didn't need to do much persuading, however, as the temptation of the free bar was a clear selling point.

Since that memorable year, our Game Fair experience continued to flourish. We will forever welcome our customers with open arms and entice with exclusive product launches, a sprinkling of wizardry from our in-house magician, and of course the temptation of a refreshingly light gin-based cocktail, kindly provided by our friends at Twelve Keys Gin. To top it all off, our specialist whizz-videographer has documented every step of the way, so you can just sit back, relax, delve into our video archives and relive the memories...

The past years have been breath-taking. We started as two childhood friends who took the plunge; now we have over 30 full-time employees, a warehouse in Portugal, numerous channels of business that range from online to shows, showroom to wholesale and new stockists flooding in.

Back in 2017 we were elated when our Imperial Explorer was crowned the winner of Best New Footwear Product of the Year at the Shooting Awards; and, most recently, Fairfax & Favor was named Best Luxury Brand of The Year at the 2019 Direct Commerce Awards.

Our Breast Cancer Care campaign is our chance to give a little something back for a cause that has touched both our family's.

We are utterly overwhelmed with the continued support this campaign receives, heavily endorsed by bloggers and celebrities and cheered on by our incredibly loyal customers. Thanks to you, to date we have raised a staggering £509,000 for the charity.

From rickety beginnings in a bedraggled pop-up gazebo plopped in a field come rain or shine, our journey on the show circuit has helped shape who we are, and what we believe in today. Our remarkable, hard-working show team are now a dab hand on the circuit, demonstrated by their fabulous accolade, winning a Gold award for Best Trade Stand at the prestigious Badminton Horse Trials."

*Story courtesy of fairfaxandfavor.com/pages/about-us

Isn't that a great story? Don't you feel like you know these guys, even if you'd never heard of Fairfax and Favor before today? Doesn't this story draw you in and introduce their brand, values and sense of fun?

Now I want you to think about your own business. What was the catalyst that got you started? Why did you decide to do this particular thing? What obstacles did you come across and how did you overcome them? What disasters have you had? What successes have you had?

Write or type your story in full as in the example above. Aim for around 2,000 words (the example above is 2128 words). This story can then be broken down into smaller bits that you can share on social media posts like I have done in the following examples…

Behind every brand is an untold story and ours is no different... except to say our story is a little different. Late in the spring of 2012, our yet-to-be founders, Marcus & Felix, made an ambitious pact: to combine their middle names and launch their very own footwear brand; one that would specialise in luxury boots and shoes inspired by country life. They wanted to pioneer rural vogue accessories and, despite having no idea how, nothing was going to stop them. Fairfax & Favor was their future. To find out what happens next please visit our blog...

We will forever welcome our customers with open arms and entice with exclusive product launches, a sprinkling of wizardry from our in-house magician, and of course the temptation of a refreshingly light gin-based cocktail, kindly provided by our friends at Twelve Keys Gin

To us, the Game Fair is more than just a show. It is a milestone, one that overcomes us with a monumental sense of pride and achievement. Find out what we've been up to on our blog...

Can you see that by taking little snippets from your story you can make engaging posts that will entice your social media audience to want to know more and therefore will visit your blog or website which gives you fabulous free traffic and eyes on your offers.

In conclusion, storytelling is an effective marketing strategy because it connects with people on an emotional level, engages and captivates their attention, helps businesses differentiate themselves, builds trust and authenticity, fosters brand recall, and has the potential to go viral. By leveraging the power of storytelling, businesses can create a compelling narrative that resonates with their audience, leaving a lasting impression and driving meaningful connections.

8 the psychology of engagement

The psychology of engagement involves understanding the underlying factors that influence customer behaviour and leveraging them to create meaningful connections. By delving into the psychological principles that drive engagement, small businesses can develop strategies that effectively capture attention, foster participation, and build long-term relationships with their target audience. I've included a list below, but don't worry if it seems a little hard to understand at first as I've included some real-life examples below which will explain the concepts.

Here are some key aspects of the psychology of engagement in marketing strategies for small businesses:

1. Attention and Perception: Small businesses need to understand the limited attention span of consumers and the selective nature of their perception. To engage effectively, businesses must create marketing materials that stand out and capture attention quickly. Utilising compelling visuals, intriguing headlines, or provocative questions can help grab attention and make a strong first impression.

2. Emotional Appeal: Emotions play a vital role in decision-making as we have already discussed. Small businesses can leverage emotional appeal by tapping into customers' desires, needs, and aspirations. By understanding their target audience's emotions and values, businesses can create marketing campaigns that resonate on an emotional level, fostering a sense of connection and empathy.

3. Cognitive Dissonance: Cognitive dissonance refers to the discomfort experienced when individuals hold contradictory beliefs or attitudes.

Small businesses can utilise this psychological principle by highlighting the gap between customers' current state and their desired state. By presenting their products or services as the solution to alleviate this dissonance, businesses can engage customers by offering a way to resolve their inner conflicts.

4. Social Proof: Humans have a tendency to rely on social proof when making decisions. Small businesses can leverage this by showcasing positive testimonials, customer reviews, or case studies that demonstrate the effectiveness and value of their offerings. By providing evidence of others' positive experiences, businesses can create a sense of trust and credibility, encouraging potential customers to engage.

5. The Power of Reciprocity: This is my personal favourite. Reciprocity is a social norm where people feel compelled to return a favour when one is given. Small businesses can tap into this psychological principle by offering something valuable to their audience, such as free content, exclusive discounts, or personalised recommendations. By providing value upfront, businesses can trigger a sense of indebtedness and encourage customers to engage further with their brand.

6. Personalisation and Relevance: Customers are more likely to engage with marketing messages that feel personalised and relevant to their needs

and preferences. Small businesses can collect customer data and utilise it to deliver tailored experiences, personalised recommendations, or targeted marketing campaigns. By demonstrating an understanding of their customers' individuality, businesses can foster a sense of connection and increase engagement.

7. Gamification and Interactive Experiences: People are naturally drawn to challenges, competition, and interactive experiences. Small businesses can incorporate elements of gamification into their marketing strategies to increase engagement. This can include interactive quizzes, contests, or rewards programs that incentivise customers to participate and stay engaged with the brand.

By incorporating these psychological principles into their marketing strategies, small businesses can create engaging experiences that capture attention, resonate emotionally, and foster long-term relationships with their audience. Understanding the psychology of engagement allows businesses to connect with customers on a deeper level, resulting in increased brand loyalty, customer satisfaction, and business growth.

Let's now look at each of the above points in a little more detail and put them into context for you so that you can see how they work in real life.

First let's look at attention and perception. We have to accept that the attention span of individuals is so limited that if we don't attract their attention immediately, they will have scrolled past, and you will have missed your window of opportunity to get them to engage with you. You need something that is going to stop them in their tracks as they are scrolling through their feeds.

Bright and attractive images are great for stopping the scroll. Recent research by Meta has shown that images of paradise do particularly well at attracting not only attention, but also likes. This is perhaps not that surprising when you consider the images are not only bright and colourful but also conjure up feelings of calm and tranquility. It is also probably worth noting that there are not many images of paradise on social media these days, so it will also be something different from the norm, and anything that interrupts a usual pattern will attract the brain's attention.

The job of the image is to stop the viewer from scrolling. The next thing the viewer will look at is that all-important first sentence of the post. The job of this first sentence is to get the viewer to read the next sentence, and to do this it must be compelling, intriguing or offer some form of curiosity.

Here are 3 examples of great scroll stopping headlines.

1. Discover the Secret to Doubling Your Productivity in Just 5 Minutes a Day!"

2. "Unlock the Hidden Strategies that Skyrocketed Sales by 200% Overnight!"

3. "Don't Miss Out on the Ultimate Guide to Mastering Your Finances and Achieving Financial Freedom!"

These first sentences, or headlines as I prefer to refer to them, offer intrigue, create FOMO (fear of missing out) or hint at secrets you're not yet aware of. Would you want to read more to find out what those secrets are? Are these sentences worthy of a second look? Would you hit the read more tab?

The rest of the post's job is to entice you to take some sort of action. The action would be determined by the outcome or objective that your marketing strategy is hoping to achieve. It could be asking your viewer to follow you on Instagram, it might be asking them to visit your blog or website, or it could be an invitation to buy something.

Now let's look at emotional appeal. This is what will get your audience to take the action you want them to take. Engaging your audience on an emotional level will be the difference between them taking action, or not.

Here is my interpretation of a typical post from a relationship coach…

Are you struggling to find the right person for you?

Do you feel left out when your friends all have partners?

Have you ever wondered why me?

If you would like help to find your perfect partner why not get in touch.

Here is my interpretation of an emotionally charged post from a relationship coach...

"Love Prevails: A Story of Hope, Healing, and Second Chances ❤️□□

In the depths of darkness, she found the strength to rise again. Meet Sarah, a woman who had weathered the storms of a painful divorce, feeling lost and questioning her worthiness of love. But little did she know that her journey was about to take an unexpected turn.

Amidst the chaos, when she least expected it, love found its way back into her life. It wasn't just any love; it was a love that mended her broken heart and filled her soul with warmth and joy once more. Mark, a compassionate soul who saw the beauty in her scars, entered her life and ignited a spark that set her world ablaze.

Together, they embarked on a journey of healing and rediscovery. Each step they took, hand in hand, was a testament to the power of resilience and the indomitable spirit of the human heart. Their love story became a beacon of hope, reminding us that love knows no boundaries and that it can bloom in the most unexpected places.

Sarah and Mark's journey teaches us that it's never too late to find true love, even after heartbreak. It reminds us that every ending is an opportunity for a new beginning. Their story is a celebration of vulnerability, trust, and the unwavering belief that happiness is possible, no matter the past.

So, to all those who have experienced the pain of divorce or the despair of lost love, hold on to hope. Your chapter of love and happiness is waiting to be written. Trust that the universe has a way of bringing the right person into your life when the time is right.

Share your own stories of love, hope, and second chances in the comments below. Together, let's inspire and uplift one another on this beautiful journey of life. ❤□□"

#LovePrevails #SecondChances #HealingHearts #NewBeginnings #LoveStory #Hope #BelieveInLove

Which coach would you be more likely to contact? Which post would you be more likely to like and comment on?

The second post is far more likely to resonate with someone as they can put themselves in Sarah's shoes and feel empathy for her. A person reading the second post would also feel that the coach is more empathetic and compassionate because this is how he/she shows up in their content.

Think about your customer. What emotions are they feeling? How can you capture those emotions in your content? Below is an example of my own…

I sat there, tears streaming down my face. Another month end and still no sign of consistent sales.

What was I going to do? How was I going to pay my bills?

I felt physically sick when I thought of the money I'd wasted on courses, coaches and books that didn't help me achieve my goals.

How was I going to tell my husband that yet again, I couldn't pay my way this month?

The more I thought about it, the harder I cried. I can still remember tasting the salt of those tears on my lips and the warmth of their tracks as they trickled down my cheeks. It was my worst day ever!

With this post I am appealing to those business owners who are experiencing the same frustration and worry that I was experiencing when I started out in business. I am showing them that I know how they are feeling because I was once where they are now. Those reading the content who are going through that experience right now will be nodding away and saying, yeah, I know how that feels. But then I do this…

Thankfully I did turn things around, so I avoided having to go back to a job I hated. It was quite by accident too. In fact, I'd been doing everything right, I just didn't know that I was missing a few pieces of the puzzle and that's what was holding me back.

Once I figured out what was missing and put those pieces in place my whole business turned around, almost overnight.

Here I'm suggesting that there is a way out of their

problem, and I've found it. I am also suggesting that it's something simple and easy to fix. My viewer would be intrigued to find out what it was that I figured out as it would probably help them too. Then I go on to reveal the solution…

It turns out I was missing opportunities in my business to capture sales. For example, I didn't have a lead generation system in place which means I was missing out on capturing those people who'd be interested in what I was selling. I had no nurture series in place to turn more of those precious leads into paying clients and I had no way of increasing the lifetime value of my clients which meant I was continually having to find new ones.

Once I plugged those holes, my business turnover increased almost immediately. I could finally stop worrying about having enough money to pay my way and cover the business bills. I could finally enjoy my business as I was no longer embarrassed by its failure to perform. I could hold my head up in front of my husband and the best thing is, he stopped asking me when I was going to get a proper job.

Here I've laid out exactly what I did to solve my problem and made it sound ridiculously simple, because, in reality, it was. I have also pointed out what solving that problem meant in terms of my own self-esteem and mental health, as well as improving my business and personal finances.

Tapping into someone's emotions is an extremely effective marketing technique, but I would advise caution. Have some moral boundaries in place otherwise you can stray into the realm of taking advantage of, or preying on the vulnerable, and that is not something I would ever encourage anyone to do.

Next, we will look at Cognitive Dissonance. I learned about this whilst studying for my Psychology degree and it is a fascinating concept. Cognitive dissonance is when someone wants to be one thing but is stuck being something else. For example, someone who wants to be a successful tennis player but finds themselves mediocre at best. A tennis coach could take advantage of this cognitive dissonance and pitch the idea that our would-be tennis star could improve significantly with a few coaching sessions.

Coaches of all walks of life also tap into this psychological tactic, myself included, because it is by far and away the most effective way of attracting new clients. If it is done ethically, it can even be said to be in the client's best interest because, after all, if they desperately want to achieve something and you can help them achieve it, it would be morally and ethically wrong to withhold that information or support.

So, let us now take a close look at my ideal client. They are about two years into their business so that they have got over the "know it all" phase and think they can do it all themself, and they have gone past the "arrogant" phase and think they are doing pretty well, even though they could be doing so much better. They are making some money, but they know they've plateaued and should be making more. They need help to grow or scale their business because nothing they are doing is working.

This tells me that the cognitive dissonance is wanting to take their business to the next level and increase their turnover, but being stuck where they are with no signs of sustainable growth. This gives me a way in with my marketing that I know will strike home with my ideal customer. I might put a post out saying something like this…

Has your business plateaued and you're not sure what to do about it?

Sam's business was doing okay, he was making good money, but he knew it could be doing so much better.

He had big plans, a holiday in Florida for the family, a new car for his wife and a new laptop for himself.

But he was being held back, because no matter what he tried his turnover just wouldn't increase.

Frustrated and annoyed he contacted me to see if I could help him overcome his obstacles.

It turned out all he needed was a shove in the right direction.

We worked together to create a solid conversion strategy that turned more of his existing leads into paying clients which meant he was able to increase his turnover without having to constantly look for new leads – how cool is that?

If you could do with a shove in the right direction, why not DM me right now and let's have a chat.

As you can see, I have tapped into the cognitive dissonance by way of a case study that shows how I helped someone in their situation overcome the obstacles that stood in their way so that they could finally increase their turnover.

Next up is social proof. We no longer trust the government, the church or the news channels, but we do still trust each other it seems. Apps like Checkatrade and Trustpilot have helped tradespeople attract more customers as they are peer reviews. The same is true of TripAdvisor and Amazon reviews. These reviews are from people who are just like us, and if they say this is okay then it must be okay.

We Brits are not great at blowing our own trumpets, but in business this becomes necessary, and you need to get comfortable doing it. You need to ask your customers to leave you a review or record a video testimonial. It can be a google review, a Facebook review, a LinkedIn recommendation or an Amazon review, the point is, it is a review that has been given by a satisfied customer, someone who is just like the person who is considering your offer.

Once you get these reviews, USE them. Put them out there on social media. Put them on the home page of your website. Share them in your emails and talk about them in your networking groups. Social proof is a great way of showing how great you are at what you do.

You can screenshot the reviews or photograph them. You can use graphic design tools such as Canva or Photoshop to edit and enhance the images or put them into branded templates so that you create a sense of congruity. The quicker your customer can recognise you online the better and the less likely they are to scroll past your post.

Put an image of the testimonial alongside some text that says how you felt when you received the feedback, or you could use it as part of a case study about that client and refer to the image in the text of the post. See an example of this below.

Glenda Shawley 🍁
Thank you **Lynne**. I've had some great connections on LinkedIn this week. I've added 17 new people and had two trending posts... first time ever. I've also had at least one booking for an event following a testimonial I shared.

Love · **Reply** · **Message** · 17 m

I could add the above as an image and then say something like this in the post…

It was an amazing feeling to receive Glenda's feedback today. Wow, TWO trending posts and at least one booking – now that's what I call a successful week.

Don't be afraid to share these testimonials and reviews as they will be the key to your success in the long run.

The next thing to consider is The Power of Reciprocity. I love this as a concept, and I've put it to the test many times over the years - and I know for a fact that it works!

Reciprocity is where you do something nice for someone and they then feel obliged to do something nice for you in return. Do you remember in Chapter Six when I talked about the one-to-ones I booked with potential clients, and I would take along a small gift. This gift not only wowed my potential client because it was a surprise and therefore unexpected, but on a psychological level, they now feel somehow indebted to me. They feel that they must do something nice for me in return for the gift.

Of course, I make no such demand of them and once the gift is given it is not talked about again (unless they bring it up), but the seed has been sown. I have just raised my chances of being the person that is chosen as their preferred supplier when they are making up their mind who to work with.

There is no need to give a physical gift either. We talked about lead magnets earlier and giving away something that is perceived as valuable to your customer. This acts in the same way as a physical gift and will achieve the same psychological outcome.

What could you give away as a gift or something that is perceived valuable to stir up those feelings of reciprocity in your potential customers? Write a list of things that you could potentially offer, both digitally and physically.

Another way of helping your customers to engage with your business is to make your marketing more personal and relevant.

Sending out emails that are generic and soulless are not going to encourage engagement but if you personalise your email by adding someone's name to it, it automatically becomes about them. There are several email service providers that you can use that will let you personalise emails that you send out en masse.

Experienced marketers will also have campaigns that are personalised based on what a person clicks on, buys, or how they respond to certain questions posed in an email chain. These email campaigns are even more likely to engage your audience as they are talking about things that are very specific to the recipient and therefore far more likely to foster interest and engagement.

Other ways of personalising the customers' experience of your business is to send out mailshots to their home address, or birthday cards, or greeting cards. Remember Joe Girard, the car salesman in Chapter One? He became the world's best car salesperson 12 years in a row by personalising his customers experience and sending out greeting cards every month to everyone who had ever bought a car from him.

Remember my little welcome pack that I post out to my customers when they sign up for my S.E.L.L. System programme? This is also a way of getting that extra engagement, they will tell others about what they received because it was unexpected and therefore different, and they will hopefully get to realise that they are more than just a client to me.

Gamification and Interactive Experiences can be a surprisingly effective way of encouraging engagement. I have personal experience of just how successful this tactic can be. Some years ago, when I was concentrating on helping my clients improve their social media, I ran 5-day challenges. People would sign up to take part in my challenge and I would run live events and training on my Facebook page for them to come along to and take part in daily.

Because I was giving them daily tasks to do, and offering feedback on those tasks, the whole challenge revolved around engagement. By the end of the 5 days people felt that they knew me and were then far more likely to engage with me on social media, visit my in-person workshops and join my paid programmes.

I have worked with clients who have run quizzes (with prizes), those who have done online Q&A sessions, some have run masterclasses and others have given TED talks, so there really is no one thing that you can do. Decide what you feel would be most useful for your customers and go with that.

To begin with it is probably pertinent to test one or two of the above-mentioned options so that you don't get overwhelmed. Which option(s) you choose will be up to you of course, but I would recommend starting with those you feel would be most beneficial to your current customer base and that fit in with your current business processes.

9 Building authentic connections

In today's fast-paced and highly competitive business landscape, small business owners face numerous challenges as they strive to establish themselves and succeed in their respective industries. Amidst the noise and digital distractions, it is easy to overlook one of the most vital elements for long-term success: building authentic connections.

Gone are the days when business transactions were solely about the exchange of goods and services. In the digital era, customers crave meaningful interactions and genuine relationships with the businesses they support. As a small business owner, your ability to foster and nurture these authentic connections can make all the difference in your venture's growth and sustainability.

This chapter delves into the profound significance of

building authentic connections and explores the various ways in which these connections can positively impact your small business. We will uncover the fundamental principles behind authentic connections, examine the benefits they bring to both you and your customers, and provide practical strategies to cultivate and maintain these connections in an increasingly impersonal world.

Authentic connections transcend mere customer transactions and delve into the realm of emotional resonance. When customers feel a genuine connection with your business, they become loyal advocates who not only repeatedly purchase your products or services but also eagerly promote them to others. These connections empower your small business to stand out from the crowd, fostering a loyal customer base that becomes your greatest asset.

Furthermore, authentic connections offer small business owners a unique advantage in an era dominated by big corporations and online marketplaces. As a small business owner, you possess the capacity to create personalised experiences, genuinely listen to your customers' needs, and adapt your offerings accordingly. By cultivating authentic connections, you establish your business as a trusted and relatable entity, capable of fulfilling the unique desires and aspirations of your target audience.

Throughout this chapter, we will explore real-world examples of small businesses that have leveraged the power of authentic connections to propel their success.

From local artisans who have cultivated devoted communities of supporters to online startups that have gone viral through genuine customer engagement, these stories illustrate the transformative potential that lies within authentic connections.

Whether you are just starting your entrepreneurial journey or looking to reinvigorate your existing small business, this chapter will equip you with the knowledge, tools, and strategies needed to foster meaningful connections with your customers. By embracing the power of authenticity and prioritising genuine human connections, you will create a thriving small business that stands the test of time and truly resonates with those you serve.

To help solidify this concept in your mind I have included some examples below of companies that have used authentic connections to build their brands and grow their businesses.

1. Patagonia: Patagonia, a renowned outdoor clothing and gear company, has built a strong and authentic connection with its customers by embodying its core values of environmental stewardship and sustainability. By consistently promoting and supporting environmental causes, Patagonia has cultivated a passionate community of supporters who align with their mission. Through initiatives like the "Worn Wear" program, which encourages customers to repair and reuse their clothing instead of buying new,

Patagonia has fostered a sense of trust and loyalty among its customers, propelling its success.

2. Glossier: Glossier, a beauty and skincare brand, has gained a cult-like following by placing an emphasis on inclusivity and engaging directly with their customers. The brand actively involves its community in product development and decision-making, seeking feedback and incorporating customer insights into their offerings. Glossier's social media presence also encourages authentic conversations, with customers sharing their experiences and recommendations. This transparent and inclusive approach has allowed Glossier to create a passionate and engaged community that fuels its growth.

3. Toms: Toms, a shoe company known for its One for One model, has leveraged the power of authentic connections to drive its success. For every pair of shoes purchased, Toms donates a pair to a person in need. This social impact-driven approach has resonated with customers, who feel a sense of purpose and connection to the brand. Toms has cultivated a loyal following of individuals who not only purchase their products but also actively promote the brand's mission, further amplifying its reach and impact.

4. Warby Parker: Warby Parker, an eyewear company, has disrupted the traditional eyewear industry by offering affordable and stylish glasses with a socially conscious twist. The company's

Home Try-On program allows customers to select and try on glasses at home before making a purchase, eliminating the hassle of traditional optical store experiences. Through a combination of thoughtful design, genuine customer engagement, and a commitment to social responsibility, Warby Parker has built a devoted customer base that appreciates the brand's authenticity and values.

5. Etsy: Etsy, an online marketplace for handmade and vintage goods, has thrived by creating a platform that celebrates independent artists and artisans. By providing a space for small-scale creators to showcase their unique products, Etsy has fostered a community of passionate buyers who value the authenticity and craftsmanship of handmade items. This authentic connection between sellers and buyers has been instrumental in Etsy's growth, allowing it to differentiate itself from larger e-commerce platforms and cater to a niche market – although in recent years it has become more Amazon than Artisan I think.

These real-world examples demonstrate how small businesses can leverage authentic connections to propel their success. By aligning with core values, engaging directly with customers, prioritising social impact, and fostering communities of like-minded individuals, these businesses have not only thrived but also created lasting and meaningful relationships with their customers.

Within my own sphere of influence, I have clients who have created wonderful communities of like-minded people that help them sell pretty much anything they can think of because those communities know, like and trust the community leader. These communities have been both online and in-person, large and small, local and world-wide.

I have also had clients who've built their business around followers on Instagram by being selective who they attract as followers and then engaging with those followers in an authentic way that resonates with that particular audience. One of those is an author who drove her Amazon and Audible sales solely through Instagram by putting out content that resonated with her intended audience, tantalised and titivated them and encouraged conversation. Another is a manufacturer of fashion and household accessories that appeal to the country pursuits community, and by using images that she knew would inspire and drive leads she was able to 5X her turnover in just one year.

Another example of authentic connection is the company GoPro. They are the people who provide the cameras for those taking part in extreme sports such as scuba diving, skiing or mountain climbing. GoPro use their marketing budget to pay their customers for video footage that they take while using their products thus providing exclusive and varied content to share on their social media platforms and website.

In Chapter Eight I told you about the success of my social media challenges, and this success came through authentic connection, my earnest desire to help other small businesses to grow by improving their social media marketing strategies. The daily tasks encouraged a two-way conversation between myself and my participants, which in turn led to a closer relationship between us. That relationship fostered trust, and the results my participants got whilst taking the challenge were the proof that I what I taught worked. Here's one of the comments I received during one of those challenges.

Shara Soraya Neal 🖐
Thank you Lynne - this last week has literally been life changing!
Can't wait for the mastermind 🙏

Now, I'm sure you'll agree, if you can change someone's life by authentically connecting with your audience, you are going to have no trouble attracting new clients, and as you can see, this lady couldn't wait to sign up for my mastermind.

Now think about how you can build authentic connections with your audience. What do you stand for? What are your ethics? What can you offer? How can you give back? How can you encourage your audience to connect with you on a more personal level in this impersonal online world that we inhabit today?

Maybe you can take some inspiration from the examples I included above, or from my clients who've built successful businesses on the back of those authentic connections, or maybe you've thought of something entirely different to entice your audience with.

To conclude this chapter, it is worth considering that in the ever-evolving landscape of small business, the importance of building authentic connections cannot be overstated. As this chapter explored, authentic connections hold the key to unlocking the true potential of your venture. They go beyond superficial transactions and forge meaningful relationships with customers, ultimately leading to loyalty, advocacy, and sustainable growth.

Authentic connections empower small business owners to stand out amidst the noise and competition, and as you are by now aware, standing out is one of my cornerstones of business growth. By cultivating genuine relationships, you create an emotional resonance that sets you apart from larger corporations and impersonal online platforms. Your ability to provide personalised experiences, listen attentively to customer needs, and adapt accordingly becomes your greatest asset. Authenticity becomes your superpower, allowing you to cater to the unique desires and aspirations of your target audience.

Moreover, authentic connections foster a sense of trust and credibility, as I demonstrated with the success of the social media challenge at bringing in new clients. When customers feel a genuine connection with your business, they not only become loyal patrons but also passionate advocates. They eagerly share their positive experiences, recommend your products or services to others, and champion your brand with unwavering support. This organic word-of-mouth marketing becomes an invaluable asset for your small business, amplifying its reach and impact far beyond your immediate circle of influence.

In a world where digital interactions often dominate, authentic connections bring back the human element. Small business owners have a unique advantage in creating personal connections, engaging in meaningful conversations, and truly understanding their customers. By prioritising authenticity and building connections based on trust, empathy, and shared values, you create a community of customers who see you as more than just a transaction. You become a relatable and trusted entity, serving as a partner in their journey and fulfilling their needs with a level of care and attention that larger organisations struggle to replicate.

As you continue on your entrepreneurial journey, remember that the importance of authentic connections transcends profit margins and revenue growth. It is about creating a business that resonates deeply with the people you serve. It is about building a legacy of trust, loyalty, and positive impact. By embracing the power of authenticity, nurturing genuine relationships, and consistently delivering value, you can forge a path towards long-term success as a small business owner.

So, take the insights, strategies, and examples shared in this chapter to heart. Cultivate authentic connections with your customers, celebrate your unique identity, and make a meaningful difference in the lives of those you serve. As you do so, you will witness your small business flourish and thrive in ways you never thought possible.

.

10 The power of visuals and multi-media

In today's visually driven and media-rich world, the way we consume information and engage with content has undergone a remarkable transformation. As a small business owner, it is essential to recognise and harness the power of visuals and multimedia in your marketing efforts. These dynamic and immersive tools have the potential to captivate your audience, leave a lasting impression, and elevate your brand to new heights of success.

This chapter explores the profound impact that visuals and multimedia can have on your small business marketing strategies. We will delve into the reasons why embracing these elements is crucial in the modern business landscape and uncover the numerous benefits they offer. From capturing attention and conveying messages more effectively to building brand recognition and fostering emotional connections, visuals and multimedia possess the potential to revolutionise your marketing approach.

In a world where attention spans are limited, to say the least, and competition for consumer attention is fierce, visuals and multimedia offer a powerful means of cutting through the noise and leaving a lasting impression. Studies consistently show that human brains process visual information significantly faster than text, making visuals a potent tool for grabbing attention and conveying messages in a concise and impactful way. By incorporating visually engaging elements into your marketing materials, such as eye-catching images, videos, infographics, and interactive content, you can instantly capture your audience's interest and make a memorable impact.

Furthermore, visuals and multimedia have the unique ability to evoke emotions and forge connections with your target audience. Through carefully crafted visuals, you can tap into the power of storytelling, using images and videos to convey narratives, spark curiosity, and elicit emotional responses. These emotional connections deepen the bond between your small business and your customers, fostering brand loyalty, advocacy, and a genuine sense of community.

Moreover, embracing visuals and multimedia enables your

small business to showcase its unique personality and differentiate itself from competitors. With the rise of social media platforms and visual-centric platforms like Instagram and TikTok, businesses now have unprecedented opportunities to showcase their products, services, and brand identity through visually compelling content. By leveraging the creative potential of visuals and multimedia, you can create a distinct and memorable brand image, cultivate an engaged online following, and stand out in a crowded marketplace.

This chapter will guide you through the practical strategies and best practices for integrating visuals and multimedia into your small business marketing efforts. We will explore the various platforms and mediums available, examine case studies of small businesses that have successfully leveraged visuals, and provide actionable tips to create visually stunning and engaging content on a limited budget.

By embracing the power of visuals and multimedia, you can elevate your small business marketing to new heights, effectively communicate your brand message, captivate your audience, and forge lasting connections. So, let us embark on this journey to unleash the transformative potential of visuals and multimedia in your small business marketing endeavours.

It is worth noting that individuals have their own preferred way of taking in information. This is especially true in learning. Since we are, as business owners, often trying to convey information that the consumer would need to take in and process it is worth thinking about how you present this information so that you are not inadvertently limiting who will access it.

A visual learner is an individual who comprehends and retains information most effectively through visual aids and visual stimuli. These learners have a natural inclination to process and understand information presented in the form of images, diagrams, charts, graphs, videos, and other visual representations.

The characteristics of a visual learner can vary from person to person, but there are some common traits often associated with this learning style. Visual learners tend to gravitate towards textbooks, charts, maps, diagrams, and other visually appealing resources. They find it easier to understand complex concepts when they are presented with visual aids that organise and illustrate information.

An audio learner is an individual who learns and absorbs information most effectively through auditory means. These learners have a preference for processing information through listening and verbal communication. They rely on spoken words, sounds, and voice inflections to understand and retain information.

Here are some key characteristics associated with audio learners. Audio learners have a natural ability to process and interpret information through listening. They excel at understanding spoken language and picking up on verbal cues, such as tone, pitch, and rhythm. They may have a knack for remembering information heard in lectures, discussions, or audio recordings such as podcasts.

A kinaesthetic learner, also known as a tactile learner or hands-on learner, is an individual who learns and retains information most effectively through physical experiences and active involvement. These learners have a preference for engaging their sense of touch and body movements to understand and process new information.

Here are some key characteristics associated with kinaesthetic learners. Kinaesthetic learners thrive when they can actively participate in the learning process. They prefer activities that involve physical movement, manipulation of objects, and direct engagement with the subject matter. They learn best through firsthand experiences rather than passive observation.

Now that you know, and hopefully understand that different people engage with information and learning in different ways, I hope you can see the benefit of producing your content in different formats.

For example, a visual learner will absorb your information best if it is presented in video format. An auditory learner would prefer a podcast and a kinaesthetic learner would prefer something like a challenge or step-by-step instructions.

Don't worry if, up until this moment, you have only ever

published text-based posts with perhaps one image, as the rest of this chapter is going to devote itself to the "how" of multi-media creation and presentation.

First let's take the visual learner and see what we can create to satisfy their preferred style of learning and information gathering…

The first thing that springs to mind is video. But creating videos can be very unsettling if you've never done anything like this before. Here's the advice my coach gave me all those years ago when I started out on my online marketing journey…

"Record yourself every single day for 90 days Lynne. Record a one-minute video, it doesn't matter what it's about, it can be your shopping list for all I care, the point is, you need to learn to get over yourself and be able to record a video confidently as this will be a crucial tool in your marketing arsenal".

So there you have it. I found that I'd "got over myself" after about 30 days of recording myself. I stopped worrying about what I sounded like, that my accent was awful, that my mouth looked wonky when I spoke and that I said "so" quite a lot. It got to the point where I actually stopped watching them back because I'd got so fed up of myself. But the goal was achieved, I could produce videos at will without breaking out into a cold sweat or vomiting into the wastepaper basket underneath my desk.

I would advise you get used to doing everything in one take otherwise you will need editing tools and all manner of expensive equipment – plus you won't ever get anything out there because you will be forever tinkering with it to make it perfect.

Another tip is to livestream to your Facebook page or group. This way you will just do it and not worry too much about silly little mistakes that you make, which don't matter by the way.

Tools that I have found useful for videos are:

My smartphone. Mine is an iPhone but any phone these days is just as good.

My laptop. The camera in my laptop is pretty good and can record decent videos.

Zoom. You can create a free account and record a meeting for up to 40 minutes (the meeting can just be you and this is how I've recorded most of my training videos and webinars). The paid version is just £14 per month and lets you record for as long as you wish.

OBS. This is far more sophisticated, and you need to know what you're doing with it, but it is free and you can edit your videos here too. You need to download the software to your laptop or computer to be able to use it.

Another great way to attract a visual learner is by creating an infographic. This is a visual representation of a concept. I've included one I made earlier for illustration. It talks you through the 4 steps of my S.E.L.L. System in a visual way.

I created it on a tool called Canva and you can find it at canva.com. At the time of writing this book you could set up a free account, but for just £10 a month I would encourage you to upgrade as you get access to thousands of free images, graphics and templates. I used one of their templates to create the infographic below.

Graphs, charts, Venn diagrams and flowcharts can also be a great way of encouraging visual learners to consume your information and these can be created for free on Microsoft Word. Just hit the insert button on your tools ribbon at the top of your screen (see the image below) and you'll see there is an option for "Chart" (graphs and so on) and "SmartArt" (flow diagrams etc). This is a completely free way to generate some great visual content.

An audio learner would prefer to listen to their content rather than view it so you need to think of ways that you can get audio versions of your content in front of that audience. One simple way is to use Zoom. Once you've finished recording Zoom will provide an audio file in addition to the video file. You can add this to your social media posts, website or emails for them to download and listen to whenever is convenient.

Podcasts were a thing, but they have become too difficult to monetise for most small businesses and they are now becoming less popular as a way of engaging an audience. However, if you want to stand out and be the small business that focuses on Podcasts, I would encourage you to do so, but you must acknowledge that you're going to need to invest in some good recording equipment. There are many platforms to host your podcast with, Spotify or iTunes being obvious choices for many podcasters.

It is also worth noting that if you want to attract audio learners the social media platform to be on would be Clubhouse. This is a social media channel that is made up of various "rooms" that host various discussions on various topics. Although it was quite quick to take off, its number of users has now declined as again, it has proven more difficult to acquire clients through it.

Kinaesthetic learners need activity. Quizzes, challenges, recipes, guides and YouTube tutorials are what these learners crave. They take in information by "doing". If you can think of ways to engage this audience in some kind of activity you can have them eating out of your hand in no time.

Challenges are definitely something to consider but they are time-consuming to run (as I well know) and they are expensive to promote as you will most likely need hundreds of people to make it viable and fun for everyone, so you will need some sort of paid campaign to bring in the participants. You will then need to consider what you are going to get them to do, how they are going to do it and how you are going to hold them accountable or give them feedback.

My social media challenges ran for five days but I was promoting them for two weeks beforehand, I had a welcome live-stream the Saturday before we started and a "get ready" livestream on the Sunday. I then had to be up at 6am each morning to make sure my daily task had been posted and then be available for the whole day to answer questions and give feedback on the tasks.

I also had to prepare all the prompts, email reminders and text messages that were needed to make the whole thing run smoothly. Challenges are a great way to engage with your audience, foster relationships and showcase your expertise, but they are not necessarily cost effective when you factor everything in.

Quizzes can be fun and engaging for kinaesthetic learners as they offer the participant a chance to do something rather than just read something. A quiz that was run by one of my clients, who was a photographer, was particularly memorable. She ran a quiz on Instagram that offered free professional headshots to anyone who could find AND PHOTOGRAPH the answers to her questions. The photographs then had to be uploaded to Instagram with a specific hashtag and the photo had to include her company's tag. It created a lot of buzz around her brand and got her name out to people who would never otherwise of heard of her. She also secured 6 months' worth of business out of that one quiz.

YouTube videos are always the go-to for kinaesthetic learners because they allow you to take action while learning. They can simply watch what happens on the screen and copy the actions. People have learnt to paint, cook, practice yoga and even train their dogs while watching YouTube. Don't underestimate this channel as a way to engage your audience.

YouTube is free to use and simple to upload your videos to. You can choose whether you want to make them public (anyone can see them) or private (only those who have the link can see them). You can't record your videos on YouTube, you must record them on another device and then upload them afterwards. Once they are uploaded YouTube will turn them into high-definition videos for you to share across social media, in your emails or on your website.

Whilst we have concentrated on the online world there are also ways of engaging your audience in the real world too. Books are a great example for those visual learners, and you can self-publish using Amazon's Kindle option. I would, however, seek expert advice before doing anything because, as with most things, there are minefields and potholes that you need to avoid that you won't even know exist. I was amazed at just how much there was involved in writing, editing and publishing a book when I started out on my venture to write this one.

Leaflets are another great visual aid and can be created and printed using the Canva tool I mentioned earlier. Their printing is professional, and they are competitively priced. I have had several things printed to hand out at my networking events and to give away at my one-to-one meetings.

How-to guides are great for kinaesthetic learners, and I've given so many of these away over the years at the end of my workshops and I've received some wonderful feedback at how much easier it was with a guide to follow. Simple illustrations and step-by-step instructions were all it took.

We cannot leave this chapter without mentioning AI. With the ability to write eye-catching headlines, create captivating copy, research information and statistics, and all in a matter of seconds, ChatGPT is definitely worth a look. It does, however, have its limits as it does not know anything after 2021 and if it doesn't know for sure, it can spin quite a convincing yarn. But that said, I would advocate the use of technology wherever you can as it is likely to improve performance, increase productivity and save you a whole load of time.

Images are also now able to be created by AI and I'm sure you've also heard that music and film are also not safe from its ever-growing tentacles. Use it wisely, check your facts, be careful with copyright etc and you should be okay.

In conclusion then, the dynamic landscape of small business marketing, visuals and multimedia have emerged as powerful tools that can elevate your brand, captivate your audience, and drive success. Throughout this chapter, we have explored the myriad ways in which visuals and multimedia can revolutionise your marketing approach and enhance the connection between your small business and your target audience.

Visuals possess the remarkable ability to grab attention and convey messages with impact. They allow you to communicate complex ideas quickly and effectively, catering to the diminishing attention spans of modern consumers. By incorporating eye-catching images, videos, infographics, and interactive content, you can create memorable and engaging experiences that leave a lasting impression on your audience.

Moreover, visuals and multimedia foster emotional connections and forge deeper bonds with your customers. Through storytelling and visual narratives, you can tap into the power of emotions, sparking curiosity, empathy, and relatability. These emotional connections form the foundation of brand loyalty, advocacy, and a sense of community, leading to long-term relationships with your customers.

Visuals and multimedia also enable you to showcase your unique brand identity and differentiate yourself from competitors. In an era dominated by social media and image-centric platforms, visually compelling content can help you stand out in a crowded marketplace. By leveraging the creative potential of visuals, you can create a distinct and recognisable brand image, attract a devoted following, and leave a lasting imprint in the minds of your customers.

Furthermore, embracing visuals and multimedia allows you to adapt to evolving consumer preferences and communication trends. With the rise of video content, live streaming, virtual reality, and augmented reality, small businesses have an unprecedented opportunity to engage their audience in innovative and immersive ways. By staying abreast of these technological advancements and embracing new mediums, you can demonstrate your willingness to evolve with the times and meet your customers' changing expectations.

As a small business owner, it is crucial to recognise the transformative power of visuals and multimedia in your marketing efforts. By integrating visual elements, telling compelling stories, and leveraging new mediums, you can create an engaging and immersive experience that resonates with your audience, amplifies your brand message, and drives business growth.

So, take the knowledge, insights, and strategies shared in this chapter and apply them to your small business marketing endeavours. Embrace the power of visuals and multimedia, experiment with new technologies, and create content that sparks emotion, captures attention, and fosters a genuine connection with your target audience.

By doing so, you will unlock the full potential of visuals and multimedia to propel your small business towards lasting success in today's dynamic marketing landscape.

11 interaction and feedback

In this chapter, we embark on a journey that explores the paramount significance of interaction and feedback in cultivating meaningful connections with your target audience. As a small business owner, you possess the unique advantage of fostering a close-knit community, allowing you to engage directly with your customers in a way that larger corporations can only envy.

The era of one-sided marketing strategies has long since passed, making way for a more inclusive and interactive approach to business. In this modern landscape, customers seek genuine connections and personalised experiences. The ability to actively listen, respond, and adapt to their needs creates a profound impact on brand loyalty, customer retention, and overall success.

Throughout this chapter, we will delve into the multifaceted benefits of embracing two-way communication channels, empowering you to harness the untapped potential that lies within your audience. From harnessing the power of social media platforms to nurturing an online community, we will explore various avenues that encourage meaningful conversations and enhance the overall customer experience.

Moreover, we will emphasise the indispensable role of feedback in honing your products or services, refining your business strategies, and continuously improving your brand's offerings. Feedback serves as the compass that guides your entrepreneurial journey, directing you towards greater heights by illuminating both your strengths and areas for improvement.

Drawing from real-world examples, expert insights, and actionable tips, this chapter aims to equip you with the knowledge and tools necessary to build a thriving ecosystem of engaged customers. By the time you reach the end, you will understand the true essence of interaction and feedback as invaluable assets that can set your small business apart in an ever-competitive marketplace.

So, ready yourself to unlock the immense potential that

awaits when you prioritise meaningful connections with your audience. Let us delve into the boundless opportunities that arise when you embrace interaction and feedback and witness the transformational impact it can have on your small business journey.

Harnessing the power of social media platforms

In this digital age, social media has emerged as an indispensable tool for small business owners to connect with their audience on a global scale. These platforms offer unparalleled opportunities to foster engagement, build brand loyalty, and amplify your business's reach. To effectively harness the power of social media while encouraging meaningful interactions with your audience, consider implementing the following strategies:

1. Define Your Target Audience: Understand who your target audience is, what they value, and which social media platforms they frequent the most. For example, I use LinkedIn as my chosen channel, as this is where businesspeople hang out online. My audience is looking for advice and guidance on how to grow their business. My client who makes fashion and household accessories for those who enjoy country pursuits uses Instagram as she is able to showcase her products to an audience she has carefully cultivated and show them examples of her beautiful products. Part one of this book covered how to identify your ideal client and nail your niche, so if you're still unsure please go and re-read it.

2. Create Compelling Content: Craft visually appealing and compelling content that aligns with your brand's voice and values. Utilise a mix of engaging posts, informative articles, eye-catching images, videos, and user-generated content to keep your audience interested. For example, I use infographics, videos, live events and information posts to engage my audience so that they get to know me on a more personal level. I also share testimonials that my clients provide and stories (or case studies) to illustrate what they have been able to achieve as a consequence of implementing my methods and techniques.

3. Be Consistent and Active: Regularly post fresh content to maintain relevance and visibility. Consistency is key to building a loyal following. Develop a content calendar to plan and schedule posts in advance. I have a one-pager on my notice board that simply says what I am going to do each day. This way I can maintain consistency without having to constantly come up with ideas on the hoof.

4. Respond Promptly: Actively monitor your social media channels for comments, messages, and mentions. Respond to inquiries and feedback promptly, showing your audience that you value their input and are attentive to their needs. You will know yourself, if you've messaged someone and they don't get back to you within 24 hours you are a little disappointed. Monitor all the

channels that you are using for engagement to make sure you don't miss someone's message.

5. Encourage Dialogue: Pose questions, run polls, and spark discussions to encourage audience participation. This creates a sense of community around your brand, making your audience feel involved and heard.

6. Host Live Events: Leverage live videos, webinars, or Q&A sessions to engage with your audience in real-time. Live events add a personal touch and provide an opportunity for direct interaction. I have already mentioned that I run live events and promote them on LinkedIn, and I often post to ask my audience what they would like me to cover in the next masterclass.

7. Utilise Stories and Highlights: Social media stories and highlights offer an ephemeral yet engaging way to share behind-the-scenes content, product updates, and limited-time offers. These features foster a sense of urgency and exclusivity, driving engagement. We have already given over quite a lot of time to storytelling so you should be pretty clear on what to do here.

8. Run Contests and Giveaways: Organise contests and giveaways to incentivise engagement. Encourage users to like, comment, and share your posts to increase visibility and attract new followers. Please make sure you read and follow the terms and conditions on the platform you

intend to run contests on as there are usually some very strict rules around this.

9. Collaborate with Influencers: Partner with influencers or micro-influencers within your niche to reach a broader audience. Influencers can help amplify your message and boost engagement through their dedicated fan base. This can be as simple as offering to do a talk on someone's Facebook page or in someone's group. Many people are looking for other people to help keep their own audiences engaged.

10. Monitor Analytics: Pay attention to social media analytics to track the performance of your content and engagement efforts. Analyse what resonates most with your audience and adjust your strategies accordingly.

11. Humanise Your Brand: Share authentic stories and showcase the faces behind your business. Humanising your brand helps build trust and makes it easier for your audience to connect with your mission. We have already covered the importance of being known, liked and trusted in Part One of this book so this should be fairly simple for you to implement.

12. Listen and Learn: Be open to feedback and use it as an opportunity to improve your offerings. Actively listen to your audience's preferences and pain points and let them know their opinions matter. When I started offering support with

social media, I assumed that my audience would need help with what to post and how often to post but it turns out they needed help with finding ways of managing their social media that were far less time consuming than what they were currently doing.

By implementing these strategies, you can effectively leverage the power of social media to foster engagement with your audience as a small business owner. Embrace the interactive nature of these platforms, and you'll build a loyal and enthusiastic community around your brand, leading to long-term success and growth.

Nurturing an online community

Nurturing an online community can be a powerful way to build engagement for a small business. An online community provides a dedicated space for like-minded individuals, including customers, potential customers, and brand advocates, to come together, share ideas, ask questions, and support one another. Here's how fostering an online community can enhance engagement for your small business:

1. **Sense of Belonging:** By creating an online community centered around your brand, you provide a space where people can feel a sense of belonging. This feeling of inclusion fosters emotional connections between members and

your brand, encouraging them to engage with your content and participate in discussions. This can be achieved by running a Facebook or LinkedIn group where you invite selected people with a shared interest to join and take part in discussions and live events.

2. **Customer Support and Feedback:** An online community serves as an excellent platform for customers to seek support, ask questions, and share their experiences. By being actively involved in addressing these inquiries and feedback, you demonstrate that you genuinely care about your customers' satisfaction, which, in turn, boosts engagement and loyalty. It also gives others a chance to air their views which can add value to your group as they will be subjected to a wider sphere of opinions.

3. **Knowledge Sharing and Expertise:** As a small business owner, you can position yourself and your brand as experts in your niche by sharing valuable knowledge and insights within the community. Offering helpful tips, tutorials, or industry news showcases your expertise and encourages community members to engage with your content. I've used this technique for years and continue to do so as it still works as a lead generation tool and introduction to my higher ticket offers. In fact, just 2 days ago I ran an online masterclass on lead generation for my online community.

4. **User-Generated Content:** A thriving online community often generates user-generated content (UGC). UGC, such as reviews, testimonials, or customer stories, can be an incredibly persuasive form of content for potential customers. Encourage and highlight UGC to build credibility and engage both existing and potential customers. I have already encouraged you to make use of social proof in your weekly content and share the testimonials that you receive as well as customer stories about what they've achieved after using your product or service. Brands such as Google and Apple have user-generated content as part of their marketing strategies.

5. **Exclusive Offers and Promotions:** Reward community members with exclusive offers, promotions, or sneak peeks into upcoming products or services. This creates a sense of exclusivity and encourages active engagement within the community. While working with an author recently we encouraged engagement and built a waiting list by sharing little snippets of her upcoming book. People love being the first to see something and the interest that was generated helped her sell more copies of her book when it was finally released. Large brands such as Boots and Next use this strategy to encourage loyalty from their customers.

6. **Collaborative Projects:** Involve your community in decision-making processes or collaborative

projects. Seeking their input on new products, features, or marketing campaigns not only strengthens their emotional connection to your brand but also shows that you value their opinions. Tropic is a good example of how larger brands do this; they ask their customers what they would like to see before they produce their next offering.

7. **Encouraging Advocacy:** An engaged online community is more likely to become brand advocates. When community members have positive experiences and feel a sense of belonging, they are more inclined to share their enthusiasm with their social circles, effectively becoming ambassadors for your brand. There are tools such as Trackdesk that you can use to set up affiliate links to share with your audience to encourage them to refer others to your business. By using a tool such as this you can keep track of who is sending customers your way so that you can reward them accordingly.

8. **Organic Growth:** An active and engaged online community naturally attracts new members who are interested in the topics and discussions taking place. As word-of-mouth spreads, your community can grow organically, contributing to a broader audience for your small business.

9. **Event Hosting:** Organise virtual events, webinars, or AMAs (Ask Me Anything) sessions within your community. These events provide

opportunities for real-time interactions, promoting engagement and enhancing the feeling of community. I have always used this as a way of engaging with my audience because I can have two-way conversations, answer questions, showcase my expertise and help them get to know me better all in a one-hour masterclass online.

10. **Consistency and Moderation:** To foster engagement effectively, ensure consistent communication and moderation within the community. Be responsive, create guidelines to maintain a positive atmosphere, and address any conflicts or issues that may arise promptly. It is a good idea to set community rules at the beginning rather than wait for a problem to arise. You will find that Facebook has an option for rules when you set up your group – use it.

Nurturing an online community can be a long-term strategy that builds strong relationships with your audience, creates brand loyalty, and drives growth for your small business. By providing value, support, and a sense of community, you can encourage active participation and turn your community members into brand advocates who will, in turn, help your business thrive.

It is also worth noting here that offline communities offer all of the above benefits with the added advantage of you actually being in the room with your audience. This adds a whole new dynamic to the community. People crave personal interaction and the advantages of an in-person community should definitely not be overlooked.

You can start building a community by simply attending a networking event that's local to you. Engage in the group so that everyone gets to know you and what you can do for them. Invite those you'd like to know better to join you for coffee and get to know them on a more personal level

You can also think about running your own networking events, or maybe set up a Facebook or LinkedIn group and invite people you meet at other groups to come and join you.

The indispensable role of feedback

Feedback plays an indispensable role in forming engagement for small businesses for several compelling reasons:

1. **Customer-Centric Approach:** Feedback allows small businesses to adopt a customer-centric approach. By actively seeking and listening to customer opinions, suggestions, and concerns, businesses can align their products, services, and marketing strategies with their customers' needs and preferences, ultimately leading to higher engagement. Remember when I said I assumed my customers wanted to know what to post and

when to post but it turned out they needed a way to manage their social media that wouldn't take up so much of their valuable time? I was able to create and test a strategy that took just 15 minutes a day and brought them lots of leads and new customers. That strategy changed my business and helped it grow into what it has become today, and it was only possible because of the feedback I'd received.

2. **Continuous Improvement:** Feedback provides valuable insights into areas that require improvement. Small businesses can use this information to refine their offerings, enhance their customer experience, and stay competitive in a dynamic market. Customers appreciate businesses that actively listen and evolve based on their feedback. My customers complained that they weren't technically savvy and therefore struggled to implement some of the suggestions I'd put forward. I was then able to adjust my mentorship programme to accommodate this by offering a "done with you" service. My clients no longer worry about falling behind because I'm there to help them get the tech stuff done.

3. **Enhanced Customer Satisfaction:** When customers see that their opinions matter, they feel valued and appreciated. Addressing their feedback promptly and effectively increases overall customer satisfaction, fostering a positive perception of the business and encouraging deeper engagement. I had one lady who was not

happy with my mini mastermind and said that it wasn't what she had expected and thought it would teach her more specific techniques. I replied to her email asking her what she would like to learn, specifically. I then offered her a free one-to-one session to teach her that exact thing. She was thrilled and extremely grateful.

4. **Building Trust and Credibility:** Transparently seeking and responding to feedback builds trust and credibility. Customers are more likely to engage with a business they trust, knowing that their concerns will be taken seriously and resolved, if needed. The only way I have been able to improve my offerings is to seek feedback from those who've attended my workshops, taken my masterminds or embarked on my mentorship programmes. Criticism, although sometimes difficult to hear, is good. If you take the criticism and improve then that person did you a good turn as your business will be all the better for it.

5. **Identifying Unique Selling Points:** Customer feedback can shed light on what sets your small business apart from competitors. Understanding your unique selling points enables you to highlight these strengths in your marketing efforts, attracting and engaging customers who resonate with these distinct qualities. Because I listened to my audience, I was able to come up with a unique selling point, offering to do the tech stuff with my clients rather than relying on them to do it themselves once the session was over. I have now

become known for my hands-on approach to business coaching and mentoring and I get referrals because of it.

6. **Creating Emotional Connections:** When customers see that their feedback leads to positive changes or improvements, it fosters emotional connections with the brand. These emotional ties strengthen customer loyalty and advocacy, encouraging customers to engage in word-of-mouth marketing and refer others to the business. Tesla have recently made many changes to their electric cars based on what customers had fed back to them. Woolworths, Blockbusters, MFI and many other businesses are no longer in existence because they did not listen to what their customers wanted, and so became irrelevant and abandoned.

7. **Personalisation Opportunities:** Feedback can reveal individual preferences and pain points, allowing small businesses to personalise their interactions with customers. Personalised experiences make customers feel special and encourage deeper engagement with the brand. If, for example, you know that one segment of your customers base buys one hand cream rather than another it will make more sense to send offers that relate only to their preferred choice as they would be far more likely to buy. You can mange this kind of customer interaction within your email service providers automation systems. You can send one email to the person who favours

choice 1 and a different email to the customer that favours choice 2. Having this personalisation in your marketing will massively increase your open rates, click through rates and sales conversions.

8. **Innovative Solutions:** Customers often provide innovative ideas and solutions that businesses may not have considered. Implementing these suggestions can lead to unique product offerings or services that resonate strongly with the target audience, driving engagement and interest. Lego are a great example of this. Customers have been responsible for their Minecraft addition and also the Women of NASA addition to their collections. Starbucks changed the design of their cups after running a competition and found that most of the designs were intricate hand drawn patterns. The winning entry was an intricate flower pattern, and it was used for the limited edition cup.

9. **Reduced Churn and Increased Retention:** Addressing customer feedback can help reduce churn and increase customer retention. When customers feel their concerns are heard and resolved, they are more likely to stay loyal to the business and continue engaging with its offerings. Remember the lady that wasn't happy with my mini mastermind? Deal with the problem well and you can turn that unhappy customer into a raving fan.

10. **Word-of-Mouth Marketing:** Positive feedback and exceptional customer experiences can lead to powerful word-of-mouth marketing. Satisfied customers are more inclined to share their positive experiences with friends, family, and on social media, extending the reach of the business and attracting new customers. We have already talked about standing out and going above and beyond for your customers in the last chapter. This is a great opportunity to remember how valuable that lesson was. The more exceptional your customer service the more customers you will have.

In summary, feedback serves as a compass for small businesses, guiding them towards meaningful engagement with their audience. By actively seeking, listening, and responding to customer feedback, small businesses can build trust, foster loyalty, enhance their offerings, and create an environment where customers feel valued, engaged, and excited about their relationship with the brand.

PART THREE - LEVERAGE

In the previous sections of this book, we embarked on a journey to uncover the art creating a thriving small business. We explored the transformational power of messaging, engagement, and even the way you attract the attention of your potential customers. Now, as we step into Part three, we dive deeper into the heart of sustainable growth—leveraging your leads and cultivating unwavering loyalty among your current customers.

In this section, we'll navigate the intricacies of lead generation, nurturing, and conversion. We'll unveil strategies that not only attract new prospects but also transform them into loyal customers who return, advocate and cheerlead for your brand, and fuel the engine of your success.

The landscape of business is continually evolving, and today's small business owners are presented with an array of opportunities to connect with their audience, build relationships, and harness the power of technology and data. From crafting compelling content that resonates with your target market to implementing cutting-edge digital marketing techniques, we'll explore a multitude of avenues to leverage your leads effectively.

Moreover, we'll dive deep into the invaluable treasure trove of your current customer base. These individuals have already placed their trust in your business, and by providing exceptional experiences, personalised offerings, and a commitment to their satisfaction, you can unlock their potential as brand advocates and repeat purchasers.

As we traverse the terrain of Part Three, be prepared to embark on a voyage of discovery and implementation. The strategies and insights you'll encounter are not merely theoretical; they are practical tools designed to help you increase turnover, create lasting customer relationships, and propel your small business toward new horizons of success.

So, as we journey onward, ready your sails for the voyage ahead. The seas of lead generation and customer loyalty may be unpredictable, but with the right strategies and a steadfast commitment to excellence, your small business can navigate these waters with confidence and purpose. Welcome to Part Three: Leveraging Your Leads and Loyal Customers—a chapter that holds the keys to unlocking your business's fullest potential.

12 The psychology behind lead conversion

In the dynamic realm of business, where every interaction is a potential turning point, understanding the intricacies of lead conversion goes beyond mere strategy; it delves into the realm of psychology. Welcome to Chapter Twelve, a gateway to unravelling "The Psychology Behind Lead Conversion."

In this chapter, we journey into the fascinating landscape of human behaviour, exploring the subconscious triggers, emotional nuances, and cognitive processes that shape the journey from a curious prospect to a committed customer. As entrepreneurs and marketers, grasping the psychology behind lead conversion is akin to holding the key to unlock the hearts and minds of potential clients.

From the powerful influence of social proof that sways

decisions, to the psychological impact of scarcity that fuels urgency, each principle we uncover forms a thread in the intricate tapestry of lead conversion. As we traverse this psychological terrain, we'll draw from real-world examples and psychological research, offering you a comprehensive guide to the art of persuasion.

We'll delve into the mechanisms of reciprocity that ignite the desire to reciprocate value, the authority that draws trust like a magnet, and the emotional resonance that forges unbreakable connections. Whether you're an established business seeking to refine your approach or a budding entrepreneur navigating the seas of client acquisition, the insights within this chapter will empower you to navigate the elusive realm of lead conversion with finesse.

As we peel back the layers of human decision-making and explore the interplay of cognitive biases and emotional triggers, you'll gain the tools to craft messages that resonate deeply, design experiences that captivate, and ultimately guide leads down the path of commitment. Join us in this exploration of the psychological dance between brands and potential customers and embark on a journey that leads not only to conversions but to lasting relationships built on a profound understanding of the human psyche.

To make the most of this chapter it is vital that you first consider who your ideal customer is. Having a crystal-clear notion of who you are selling to will help you implement the techniques and methods that are revealed in this chapter and get the best results from them.

It may be worth re-visiting chapter four at this point and looking again at the Bullseye Targeting Method that is outlined there. The more specific you can be about who you are targeting the more successful your marketing will be, as it will be speaking to a specific group of people about a specific problem or desire.

Now that you are clear about who your ideal customer is we can begin to peel back the layers that are holding you back and forge a path to success by leveraging the leads that you generate.

The first layer we need to uncover is cognitive bias.

Cognitive bias refers to systematic patterns of deviation from rationality or objective judgment in decision-making. These biases are often the result of mental shortcuts and information processing strategies that our brains employ to simplify complex situations. While these mental shortcuts can be helpful in many situations, such as driving your car or doing a repetitive task at work, they can also lead to errors in judgment, distorted perceptions, and irrational decision-making.

Cognitive biases can affect various aspects of our lives, including how we perceive information, interpret events, and make choices. They can influence our opinions, beliefs, and behaviours without us even realising it. These biases are deeply ingrained in human cognition and can impact individuals across cultures and backgrounds.

Here are a few common examples of cognitive biases:

1. **Confirmation Bias:** This bias involves seeking out and interpreting information in a way that confirms our preexisting beliefs or opinions. People tend to focus on information that supports their views and ignore or downplay contradictory information. We have seen lots of evidence of this since the invention of social media. Algorithms will continue to show you content that you have shown an interest in and engaged with and not show you anything that contradicts that view. We become more and more convinced that our opinion is the one that is correct and that the opinions of others must therefore be wrong.

2. **Availability Heuristic:** This bias occurs when we rely on immediate examples or readily available information to make decisions. We often overestimate the importance of information that's easily accessible in our memory. An example of this is when we decide not to do something because the last time we did it we experienced an unpleasant reaction. We will forget that the five times we did it previous to that, ended without consequence.

3. **Anchoring Bias:** Anchoring bias occurs when we rely too heavily on the first piece of information

we encounter when making decisions. This initial information, or "anchor," then influences our subsequent judgments, even if it's irrelevant. An example may be your friend's reaction to the new guy in the office. If your friend's reaction is negative, you will tend to also have a negative opinion of them even if you've had no interaction with them yourself.

4. **Hindsight Bias:** Hindsight bias, also known as the "I-knew-it-all-along" phenomenon, involves believing, after an event has occurred, that one would have predicted or expected the outcome despite not having done so beforehand. I think we can all recall examples of this bias, can't we? I knew this would happen if I tried that, or, well it's obvious isn't it, I could have told you that would happen if …

5. **Loss Aversion:** Loss aversion refers to the tendency to feel the pain of losses more strongly than the pleasure of equivalent gains. People often avoid risks to prevent losses, even if the potential gains are greater. A good example of this is when a new business owner struggles for months to get their business off the ground rather than pay someone to help them because they fear the loss of their money more than they covet the gains that that person's knowledge and experience would bring.

6. **Overconfidence Bias:** This bias leads individuals to overestimate their own abilities, knowledge, or

the accuracy of their beliefs. People tend to believe they are better than average in various tasks and less likely to experience negative outcomes. It's funny, most people I mention this to say they don't suffer from this type of bias. I would challenge this belief and ask how good a driver are you? Anyone who has been driving for more than a couple of years will not be aware of around 95% of their journey – if you're only concentrating for 5% of the time you are driving, could you really consider yourself to be a good driver?

7. **Social Proof:** Social proof bias is the tendency to rely on the actions or opinions of others as a guide for our own behaviour, especially in uncertain situations. We often look to what others are doing to determine what is appropriate or correct. I'm sure you can think of an instance when this has been true for you.

Cognitive biases can have significant implications in marketing and in guiding customers' decision-making. Understanding these biases is crucial not only for personal awareness but also for making more informed and rational decisions, both individually and in the contexts of business, policy-making, and communication.

For example, loss aversion bias is used in marketing as research has shown that people are almost 10x more likely to buy something that prevents loss than something that offers gains. Think about how you promote your products and services, do you promote the benefits in a way that prevents loss, or in a way that promises gains.

Here is an example to put it in context...

Gain: Join my mastermind and 5X your turnover in the next 12 months

Loss: Join my mastermind and learn how to save £thousands on wasted ad spend.

Confirmation bias is also used by master marketers. They will take something that their customer believes to be true and put it in their marketing to gain attention. See an example of this below...

New Study Confirms That Chocolate Is Good For You - Indulge Guilt-Free

Okay, now that we know a little more about cognitive bias and how it can affect our customers' decision-making processes it's time to look at how we can use this bias to our advantage as business owners and marketers.

The following are examples of tried and tested ways to positively influence our customers so that they are more inclined to choose us over our competitors.

Social proof: People tend to follow the crowd. When potential customers see others engaging with your product or service, they're more likely to perceive it as valuable and trustworthy. Online reviews, testimonials, and user-generated content are potent tools for leveraging social proof.

Example: Consider a small bakery that posts images of delighted customers savouring their delectable pastries on social media. This not only showcases the quality of their products but also creates a sense of FOMO (fear of missing out) in viewers, motivating them to visit the bakery and experience the treats themselves.

One of my clients used this exact method to promote their new bakery. They would take photographs of their delicious breads, pastries and cakes and showcase them on their Facebook page which encouraged engagement and curiosity. Initially we had planned for a press release to announce their grand opening, but in the end, there was no need as they had built up curiosity, trust and engagement in their local community and by opening day they had dozens of people waiting to buy from them.

Reciprocity: The principle of reciprocity asserts that people are inclined to return favours (remember, we talked about this in chapter eight). By offering something of value upfront, you trigger a sense of obligation in potential customers, increasing the likelihood of them reciprocating with a purchase.

Example: An online yoga teacher offers free video tutorials on "Top 10 Home Workouts." This establishes goodwill and positions the teacher as helpful and supportive. As a result, when the teacher introduces a paid subscription for personalised workout plans, many recipients of the free tutorials are more inclined to subscribe due to the principle of reciprocity.

My client made great use of this technique during the pandemic. She offered free yoga tutorials online and recorded some of the sessions to use as lead magnets that she could offer for free for people to follow along to at their own pace and in their own time. When the pandemic restrictions ended, and she was able to re-open her yoga studio she had an influx of new customers and most of them came because they had been following her video tutorials and online programmes.

Scarcity: People value things that are perceived as rare or limited in availability. Creating a sense of scarcity – whether real or perceived – can drive urgency and prompt action.

Example: An e-commerce store announces a limited-time "Flash Sale" with a countdown timer and a message stating "Only 10 left in stock!" This triggers a fear of missing out and encourages hesitant leads to make a purchase decision sooner rather than later.

This should, however, be used with caution because false claims can lead to adverse reactions from potential customers and negative comments on social media. That said, I've made good use of this when selling tickets to my events, workshops and masterclasses. I've reminded people that they only have 3 days left to sign up, or that there are only 5 tickets remaining.

Authority: People are more likely to trust and follow recommendations from authoritative figures or sources. Demonstrating your expertise and credibility can significantly impact lead conversion.

Example: A small consulting firm releases a series of informative videos where their experts share insights on industry trends. As these videos gain traction, the firm's reputation as an industry authority grows. This elevated credibility subsequently influences leads to choose their consulting services over competitors'.

This worked extremely well for a training company that I worked with. They put together a series of training videos and invited a celebrity to come and talk to them about the videos and the benefits to large organisations with large teams to train. The professional looking videos, coupled with the authority of the liked and trusted celebrity helped to secure many sales and propel them from obscurity to the "go-to" people for training in their sector.

Emotional Appeal: Emotions play a significant role in decision-making. Crafting marketing messages that resonate emotionally can forge a strong connection between leads and your brand. We have covered this in some depth in previous chapters so you must be familiar with this concept by now.

Example: An eco-friendly beauty product company

doesn't just highlight the effectiveness of their products. They also emphasise the positive impact on the environment and the health of families. This emotional appeal resonates with environmentally conscious leads, making them more likely to convert.

A client of mine created a range of halal skin care products that she knew would create an emotional connection with her intended audience. From day one she was inundated with orders from people looking for halal products.

By understanding and leveraging these psychological principles, you can effectively guide leads along the conversion journey. From appealing to their need for social validation to sparking emotions that resonate deeply, your strategies can tap into the intricate fabric of human psychology, turning curious leads into committed customers.

Now let us look at some offline lead generation methods that you can use where psychology also comes into play.

Networking Events:

Psychological Trigger: Reciprocity

How it Works: When you engage in meaningful conversations, share insights, and provide value to others at networking events, you trigger the principle of reciprocity. People are more likely to reciprocate your efforts by showing interest in your business or services.

Also, by referring others to their services they are more likely to want to reciprocate by referring others to you.

Examples: At a local business meetup, you discuss effective marketing strategies with fellow attendees. In return, some of them express interest in your consulting services. You refer two people to businesses within your network, those businesses then work harder to find suitable people to refer to you.

Seminars and Workshops:

Psychological Trigger: Authority

How it Works: By presenting yourself as an expert in your field during seminars or workshops, you tap into the authority principle. Attendees are more likely to trust your expertise and consider your offerings. This is a method I've used since my very first day in business. Workshops allowed me to showcase my expertise and allowed people to get to know me on a personal level.

Example: Hosting a financial literacy workshop positions you as a knowledgeable financial advisor, increasing the chances that attendees will reach out for further advice.

Community Involvement:

Psychological Trigger: Social Proof

How it Works: Active participation in community events or projects showcases your commitment to the community. This elicits social proof – when people see your positive impact, they're more inclined to support your business.

Example: Sponsoring a charity run aligns your business with a good cause and showcases your community involvement, making locals more likely to consider your products or services.

Trade Shows and Expos:

Psychological Trigger: Scarcity

How it Works: Limited-time offers or exclusive deals offered at trade shows create a sense of scarcity. Attendees are more motivated to take immediate action to avail themselves of these special opportunities.

Example: A technology company promotes a new product launch exclusively at a trade show. The limited availability prompts attendees to make purchasing decisions on the spot. Again, I've made use of this technique by offering special offers to those who attend my workshops but make it clear that the offer is for that day only.

By incorporating these offline lead generation activities and leveraging the psychological triggers, you can create meaningful connections, establish trust, and encourage potential customers to take action, ultimately driving your business's growth and success.

In the captivating journey through this chapter, we've

unearthed the profound impact that psychology wields in the realm of lead generation for small business owners. The intricate dance between human cognition and decision-making has been laid bare, revealing the subtle yet powerful forces that underpin the successful cultivation of leads.

As a small business owner, you now hold the key to leveraging psychological principles that transcend conventional marketing tactics. You've learned that behind every click, every inquiry, and every conversion lies a complex interplay of emotions, motivations, and biases. Armed with this knowledge, you're equipped to craft messages that resonate on a personal level, design experiences that captivate the senses, and build connections that transcend the transactional.

From the allure of social proof that fosters credibility to the urgency of scarcity that spurs immediate action, these psychological triggers serve as your compass, guiding potential customers along the path to becoming valued clients. Your understanding of reciprocity allows you to bestow value before even seeking commitment, fostering a sense of indebtedness that can lead to enduring loyalty.

The authority you exude as an industry expert nurtures trust, fostering relationships built on mutual respect. And when you skilfully tap into the emotional chords of your audience, your brand becomes not just a choice, but a reflection of their aspirations and values.

In the ever-evolving landscape of business, where competition is fierce and attention spans are fleeting, your grasp of psychology provides a competitive edge. You're not merely selling products or services; you're crafting narratives that resonate, building bridges that span beyond the digital divide, and fostering connections that stand the test of time.

As you step out into the world armed with these insights, remember that behind every lead lies a human being with desires, fears, and dreams. It's your understanding of these underlying human elements that transforms leads into relationships, transactions into partnerships, and curiosity into commitment.

With the psychology of lead generation as your guiding light, your journey as a small business owner becomes one of transformation – not only of potential customers into loyal advocates but also of your business into a beacon of authenticity and resonance. So, go forth, armed with the power of psychology, and watch as the seeds you sow blossom into a garden of fruitful connections, sustaining your business's growth and propelling you toward unprecedented success.

13 The power of the lead magnet

Magnetic Marketing – Harnessing the Power of Lead Magnets to Captivate Your Ideal Customers

In the ever-changing realm of business, where attention is a prized commodity and first impressions are more important than ever, the art of capturing the attention of your ideal customers becomes a potent instrument in your arsenal. Welcome to Chapter Thirteen, where we delve into the captivating realm of "Magnetic Marketing: Unleashing the Power of Lead Magnets."

In this chapter, we unravel the secret weapon that stands as a beacon to guide your potential customers toward your brand's embrace – the lead magnet. A lead magnet is not just an offering; it's an invitation, a glimpse into the world of value and expertise that you promise to provide. It's the initial handshake that begins a relationship and the spark that ignites the curiosity of your target audience.

From irresistible eBooks that share exclusive insights or engaging webinars that empower and educate, to free trials of your exclusive gym, lead magnets wield a unique influence in the world of marketing. In the pages ahead, we'll explore how these magnetic offerings have the uncanny ability to cut through the noise, arrest wandering attention, and beckon your ideal customers to step into your realm.

Through real-world examples and time-tested strategies, we'll delve into the art of crafting lead magnets that resonate deeply with your audience's needs, desires, and aspirations. We'll uncover the psychology behind why these offerings hold such allure, and how they spark the principle of reciprocity – prompting potential customers to willingly share their contact information in exchange for the value you promise.

But the journey doesn't end with a successful opt-in; that's just the beginning. We'll also guide you through the delicate dance of nurturing these new connections, of turning leads into enthusiasts, and enthusiasts into brand advocates. With the power of lead magnets at your fingertips, you hold the ability to not only capture attention but to hold it, to foster trust, and to build relationships that stand the test of time.

So, join us as we journey into the heart of "Magnetic Marketing," and equip yourself with the strategies and insights to create lead magnets that resonate, allure, and beckon your ideal customers to step into the transformative world you offer. Let's explore how, with each carefully crafted lead magnet, you don't just capture attention – you capture hearts and minds, forging connections that become the cornerstone of your business's success.

To be able to entice someone into your world you must first know what it is that they desire. What is it that they are trying to achieve, what is their secret wish? Knowing the answers to these questions will equip you to create meaningful lead magnets that your audience simply cannot resist.

A lead magnet is simply something that entices your ideal customer to put up their hand up and state that they are potentially interested in what you are offering. For example, a lead magnet for a gym may be a month's free trial period, a flower shop may offer a book on flower arranging and a business coach may offer a free video course on how to overcome imposter syndrome. It doesn't matter what the lead magnet is as much a how valuable a potential customer deems it to be.

Before we jump into lead magnets, I would first like to explain the concept of Magnetic Marketing. The idea of a magnet is that it attracts, but we must also remember that it also repels. The image below shows that we are only looking to attract those few people who truly fit our ideal client avatar.

Our lead magnet must not attract everyone but rather just those who are interested in what we are offering. For example, it would be futile to attract lots of people with a free trial in your gym if they are not really interested in joining the gym once the trial is over.

Your lead magnet should be something that is going to offer value to a potential customer and attract the type of person that you would consider your ideal client. My lead magnets tend to be aimed at new and small business owners because that is who I am trying to attract into my business. As such my lead magnets offer simple solutions to common problems that new and small business owners have such as how to grow your social media followers, how to set up an email campaign, 5 things you really need to know before you start an online business, and so on.

Think about what you could offer as an incentive for someone to try you out for free. Online lead magnets are easy as they are free to deliver and cost nothing to create other than a little time and effort, and they can be anything from checklists to "how-to" guides or video tutorials to webinars. The more value packed the lead magnet is seen to be the more people will opt into it and the more leads you will then have.

Here are some things for you to consider as lead magnets for both on and offline businesses.

Online Businesses:

1. **Ebook or Whitepaper:**

   - A digital guide that dives deep into a relevant industry topic, offering valuable insights and solutions. I have created many of these and they have always been successful lead magnets as they are value packed and my audience can see that before they opt in.

   - Example: A digital marketing agency offers an ebook titled "The Ultimate Guide to Social Media Engagement" that provides strategies and tactics for boosting engagement on social platforms.

2. **Webinar or Online Workshop:**

   - An interactive online session where you share expertise and actionable tips, often followed by a Q&A session. I run these fairly frequently and they are always well received and produce lots of new leads as they are interactive, and people know they can get their problems solved if they attend.

- Example: A fitness coach hosts a live webinar on "Healthy Habits for a Busy Lifestyle," sharing practical tips and demonstrating exercises.

3. **Email Course:**

- A series of emails delivered over a specified period, offering a structured learning experience. I have used this technique and found it to be one of the best at converting leads into paying clients. I think the fact that they are seeing me every day for a week helps to build a relationship with me and it definitely helps the know/like/trust factor as they get to try out what I recommend there and then and see the results.

- Example: A cooking blog offers a 7-day email course on "Mastering Quick and Easy Weeknight Dinners" with a new recipe and cooking tips each day.

4. **Checklist or Template:**

- A downloadable resource that provides a step-by-step guide or template for a specific task. I have produced dozens of these over the years to help with everything from gaining followers on Facebook to creating welcome series in your email campaigns. People love templates as they are simple to use and give quick and measurable results.

- Example: A productivity app offers a downloadable "Weekly Planning Checklist" that helps users organise their tasks and goals.

Offline Businesses:

1. **Workshop or In-Person Class:**

- A hands-on, interactive session held at a physical location where participants learn a new skill. I started my business by literally doing this, running online marketing workshops for local small business owners. It is a great way of getting to know people, showcasing your expertise and building relationships.

- Example: An art supply store hosts a painting workshop for beginners, teaching techniques and offering all necessary materials.

2. **Free Consultation or Evaluation:**

- A personalised one-to-one session where you assess the potential customer's needs and provide tailored recommendations. I offer a free blueprint call where I will look at ways to increase your turnover by identifying areas where you are letting sales slip through your business unnoticed.

- Example: A financial advisor offers free financial consultations to help individuals plan for their future.

3. **In-Store Event or Demo:**

- An event or demonstration held at a brick-and-mortar store to showcase products and engage with customers. Back in the day I invited new business owners to my training room to show them how to build a simple website in one morning.

- Example: A cosmetic store hosts a makeup demonstration event, offering makeup tips and allowing customers to test new products.

4. **Exclusive In-Store Discount:**

- A special discount offered exclusively to customers who visit the physical store. I gave attendees of my workshops exclusive discounts to my masterminds.

- Example: A boutique clothing store provides a "VIP Shopping Day" where customers receive 20% off on their purchases in-store.

In both online and offline contexts, the key is to offer something of value that addresses your target audience's needs or interests. The goal is to provide a taste of the expertise, products, or experiences you can offer, creating a positive impression and building a foundation for a lasting relationship with your potential customers.

Many of the examples above can be created online and for free by making use of free tools such as Microsoft Word and Excel, Canva and Designrr as well as utilising tools such as Zoom for video and audio-based lead magnets.

Discount codes and money off vouchers can be created as a printable download and you could also create a printable ticket for a free trial or limited membership offer.

Whether you choose a money off voucher or a discount will be up to you but I would recommend asking what your current customers would prefer and going with that.

As we conclude this chapter, the profound impact of lead magnets in propelling small businesses toward success becomes crystal clear. Like magnetic forces that draw objects closer, lead magnets possess an undeniable allure that captures the attention, interest, and ultimately the hearts of your target audience.

Throughout these pages, we've unveiled the artistry behind crafting compelling lead magnets – those tantalising offerings that promise a world of value and expertise. From ebooks that educate to workshops that engage, these magnets transcend mere transactional interactions, igniting a spark of curiosity that evolves into a deep and lasting connection.

But the power of lead magnets extends beyond the initial opt-in. It's a gateway to fostering relationships, nurturing leads into loyal customers, and converting customers into advocates. Through the principle of reciprocity, your gesture of providing value begets trust, laying the foundation for a journey that transforms passive onlookers into active participants in your business's narrative.

In the digital age, where attention spans are limited and competition is at an all-time high the efficacy of lead magnets in cutting through the noise cannot be overstated. They provide a means to differentiate, to resonate, and to address the precise pain points and aspirations of your audience. By offering a tangible taste of what your small business stands for, you pave the way for a future where every engagement is informed, every purchase is meaningful, and every connection is authentic.

With each lead magnet you deploy, you're not just capturing email addresses or contact information – you're capturing opportunities. Opportunities to educate, to inspire, and to build a tribe of individuals who resonate with your brand's essence. You're cultivating a garden of relationships and encouraging brand loyalty and advocacy.

As you venture forth armed with this newfound understanding, remember that lead magnets aren't just tools; they're storytellers, ambassadors of value, and catalysts of connection. They bridge the gap between your aspirations and your audience's needs, aligning them in a symphony of mutual benefit.

So, embrace the power of lead magnets as an integral part of your small business strategy. Use them not just to capture leads, but to captivate hearts and minds. And as you wield this magnetic marketing weapon, you're not just building a small business – you're shaping a legacy that resonates, endures, and flourishes in the hearts of those you touch.

14 The fortune's in the follow up

The Art of Follow-Up – Nurturing Relationships and Amplifying Conversions for Small Businesses

In the wonderful journey of small business success, the road doesn't end with the initial spark of interest. Rather, it is in the careful and deliberate follow-up that the seeds of relationships are sown, and the conversions that sustain growth take root. Welcome to Chapter Fourteen, where we delve into the art of follow up.

In this chapter, we unveil the pivotal role that effective follow-up plays in fostering relationships and maximising conversions. It's a process that goes beyond the digital or initial transaction, beyond the fleeting moment of the first sign-up. It's the bridge that leads from that initial point of contact to a deep and lasting connection with your audience.

From automated email sequences that educate and engage to personalised outreach that speaks directly to your customers' needs, follow-up strategies are the threads that weave a narrative of trust, loyalty, and mutual understanding. Whether you're guiding potential clients down the sales funnel or nurturing existing customers for repeat business, the art of follow-up is the secret ingredient that transforms casual interactions into meaningful engagements.

Through real-life case studies and expert insights, we'll explore how consistency and relevance in follow-up efforts can create a halo effect, making your brand synonymous with authenticity and value. We'll delve into the psychology of engagement, uncovering the triggers that prompt recipients to not just open your emails, but to eagerly anticipate them.

But it's not just about technology and automation – it's about the human touch, the personal connection that bridges the digital divide. We'll guide you through the delicate balance of being informative without being intrusive, offering value without overwhelming, and nurturing without pressuring. In doing so, you'll learn how to seamlessly integrate follow-up into your business's DNA, making it a cornerstone of your success.

As you embark on this exploration of the art of follow-up, keep in mind that you're not just pursuing conversions – you're cultivating relationships. You're crafting experiences that resonate, engaging in conversations that matter, and paving the way for your small business to thrive in the hearts and minds of your audience.

So, join me as we unravel the magic that unfolds after the first sign-up, and discover how the art of follow-up can be your most potent tool in building lasting relationships and amplifying conversions. Through each carefully timed email, each personalised interaction, and each meaningful touchpoint, you're not just nurturing business – you're nurturing connections that will bear the fruits of loyalty, advocacy, and sustained growth.

First Contact: Your lead magnet may be the first contact that your potential customer has with your business and so it's worth putting time and effort into it. Imagine if you were meeting that person in real life, what first impression would you want to create? How would you dress? Where would you meet that person and why that particular place?

Meeting someone through a lead magnet should be no different, but somehow it usually is. Opting into someone's newsletter or applying for a 10% discount on your first order is not what you might consider personal interaction is it? It feels purely transactional and there is no investment of emotion in that initial contact. But what if you could make it more personal? How would that impact your leads impression of your business?

One way I like to personalise my lead magnets is by

utilising the "success" or "thank you" page once someone has signed up. I don't just put the usual "thanks for signing up for my free whatever" message, I thank them for their support and assure them as a small business owner I value their support and appreciate their interest in my business. This goes right back to part one of this book where we talked about standing out, doing something different to what everyone else is doing.

Think about your lead magnet and how you can personalise that first contact. How can you stand out and do something that no one else in your industry is doing?

The next thing I do to personalise their experience is send them an email with a link to the lead magnet. The email will include their name (the one they used to sign up to the lead magnet) so that it doesn't just feel like I've sent the same email to everyone. I will thank them again for their support and interest in my business and explain what happens next. I will tell them where or how they can access the lead magnet. It may be a simple hyperlink to click, or it may be that they need to visit a physical premises to access it.

They will then be added to my welcome series (as long as they have agreed to this when they sign up as your emails need to be GDPR compliant if you are operating in Britain or Europe). A welcome series is a series of emails that continue the conversation with your lead to foster a relationship and give more value. My welcome series usually consists of 5 emails (one per day for 5 days) where

I expand on whatever was in my lead magnet.

For example, in my 5 things you really need to know before starting an online business I cover those 5 things in my initial lead magnet but over the next 5 days I cover topics that I know will interest them such as how to go from unheard of to sold out in 30 days, how to create compelling headlines that your customers won't be able to resist and what the biggest obstacle in their business is right now, and how to overcome it.

Here's how that works...

After requesting a copy of my lead magnet they get an email with a link to access the video training (I prefer to video my training as it just means I can cover more in less time).

My lead accesses the lead magnet and learns all the things I promised in my promotion – the 5 most common things my clients wished they'd known before starting their business.

The next day I send them another email which thanks them again for their interest in my lead magnet and a reminder of the link in case they didn't get a chance to view it. I then go on to talk to them about what they can do to promote their offers to go from unheard of to sold out in 30 days. At the end of the email I tell them that tomorrow I will share ow to get your offer spot on so that your ideal customers will be queuing up to work with you – something to entice them to look out for the next email from me.

The next day they get the email I promised yesterday, training on how to get their offers noticed and taken up by their ideal clients. Again, in this case it is a video tutorial as these are a great way of helping clients get to know the real you. At the end of the email I tell them what to expect from me in tomorrow's email.

The next day is another video tutorial on how to convert more of your leads into paying customers and the day after that a video that promises to reveal the biggest obstacle in your business right now and how to overcome it.

As I mentioned earlier, I chose these particular topics because they are the ones that are most commonly mentioned when I talk to small business owners about what they wished they had known before committing to starting a small business – and I wish I'd know about them too as they would have saved me a whole load of time, money and effort. You will obviously choose things that relate best to your audience.

After 5 days of nurturing my new leads, I ask them if they would like to book a free call with me to discuss their business growth needs and create a personalised blueprint. A few will take me up on the offer, but most will not. For those that don't I add them to my ongoing nurture series where I email them once a week and give them hints, tips and ideas to help them build, grow or scale their business or share behind the scenes of what's happening in my business or tell stories of how I was once where they are now and how I got from there to where I am now.

I've had people on my list for months before they've bought from me, and one man took 2 years to get in touch and ask for my help. Some people never buy from me, and I eventually remove them from my list – and that's okay, I can't help everyone and I'm not everyone's cup of tea, I guess.

It is the consistency of contact that will win over your leads and turn them into paying clients. Over time they get to know you, like you and trust that what you are saying makes sense and works for them. This trust takes time and it's no good trying to rush things as you will just end up with lots of unsubscribes.

Consistency and relevance in follow-up efforts can indeed create a halo effect that establishes your brand as synonymous with authenticity and value. Let's delve into how this dynamic unfolds:

1. Consistency Creates Reliability: When your follow-up efforts are consistent, whether through regular newsletters, timely responses, or scheduled updates, you showcase your commitment to your audience. Consistency breeds reliability, and reliability cultivates trust. By consistently delivering valuable content and staying in touch, you become a reliable source of information and support, positioning your brand as one that can be counted on.

2. Relevance Demonstrates Understanding: Relevance in your follow-up communications shows that you understand your audience's needs, preferences, and pain points. When you tailor your messages to address their specific interests, challenges, and aspirations, you demonstrate that you're not just broadcasting generic content – you're genuinely invested in their well-being. This level of personalisation fosters a deeper connection and makes your audience feel valued.

3. Combined Impact: The Halo Effect: When consistency and relevance intertwine, they create a powerful synergy known as the halo effect. Your consistent presence builds familiarity, while your relevant content demonstrates understanding. This combination enhances your brand's image, casting a halo of credibility and authenticity. Your audience begins to associate your brand with dependable information and insights that align with their needs.

4. Building Authority and Expertise: Consistency and relevance bolster your brand's authority and expertise within your industry or niche. By consistently sharing valuable insights and solutions, you position yourself as a knowledgeable resource. Over time, your audience starts to see you as an expert, further amplifying the halo effect. As your brand becomes synonymous with reliable guidance, customers and prospects alike are drawn to your offerings.

5. Emotional Connection: The halo effect extends beyond the logical realm into the emotional. When your consistent and relevant follow-up efforts resonate emotionally, you tap into a deeper level of connection. People are more likely to engage with brands that evoke positive emotions and make them feel understood. This emotional resonance strengthens the halo effect, fostering loyalty and advocacy.

6. Long-Term Relationships: As the halo effect takes hold, your brand transforms from a transactional entity to a trusted partner. The consistency and relevance of your follow-up efforts have nurtured relationships that go beyond immediate transactions. Customers begin to perceive your brand as a genuine ally, making them more likely to remain loyal over the long term.

In essence, the interplay of consistency and relevance in your follow-up efforts creates a positive feedback loop. The more consistent and relevant your communications, the stronger the halo effect becomes. This effect permeates your audience's perception of your brand, resulting in a reputation for authenticity, value, and commitment. As you continue to uphold these principles, you lay the foundation for enduring customer relationships, sustained growth, and a brand that stands out in a crowded marketplace.

Having somewhere to host your list and create your email campaigns and automations is crucial in today's business world. Your list is yours, you own it, you control it and no one can take it away from you. Unlike your social media accounts that can be suspended or shut down permanently without explanation, your email list is there for as long as you need it and if you provide value and build a relationship with that list it will become your businesses biggest asset.

There are many great email service providers and I have mentioned some in previous chapters but the ones I tend to recommend are Mailerlite (because it lets you create automated emails without having to upgrade, or at least it did at the time of writing this book), ActiveCampaign (because of its ease of use and ability to create quite complex automations that can fully support your personalisation efforts) and ThriveCart (because of its integration with payment gateways to make selling direct from your list so much easier).

As we draw the curtains on this chapter, the resounding importance of following up with and leveraging leads emerges as a cornerstone in the grand tapestry of building a successful and sustainable business. The journey from initial contact to enduring relationships isn't a linear path; it's a symphony of interactions, each note contributing to the harmonious composition of success.

Throughout these pages, we've explored the delicate art of follow-up, a journey that extends far beyond the first interaction. It's a journey fuelled by consistency, where each touchpoint reinforces your commitment and reliability, creating a foundation of trust that withstands the test of time. It's also a journey of relevance, where every message reflects a deep understanding of your audience's needs, creating a resonance that transcends transactional engagement.

The act of following up isn't merely a mechanical process; it's an emotional connection. It's the moment when potential leads transform into valued relationships, when trust is nurtured and loyalty is cultivated. The value you provide in your follow-up communications isn't just about information; it's about showing that you care, that you're invested in their success and well-being.

In an era where attention spans are short and options are abundant, the act of consistent and relevant follow-up becomes a differentiator. It's a testament to your dedication to go beyond the sale, to guide your audience on a journey of growth and empowerment. It's an investment in relationships that lead to word-of-mouth referrals, repeat business, and a loyal customer base.

Remember that your follow-up efforts are the threads that weave the fabric of your brand's identity. Each thoughtful email, each personalised message, and each touchpoint contribute to the narrative you're crafting. By infusing these interactions with authenticity, value, and empathy, you're not just nurturing leads; you're nurturing the very essence of your business.

As you step forward armed with the insights from this chapter, remember that success isn't measured solely by transactions; it's measured by the quality of connections you forge. By embracing the art of follow-up and nurturing, you're creating a legacy of lasting relationships that transcend fleeting trends and economic shifts.

So, go forth with the understanding that your follow-up efforts are bridges that lead from curiosity to commitment. Let each interaction be a testament to your brand's ethos and let each relationship you nurture be a beacon that guides your business toward a future of prosperity, sustainability, and significance.

15 Leveraging your audience – the key to increasing sales

In the dynamic world of business, where strategies constantly evolve and markets shift, the concept of leveraging an audience has emerged as a game-changing force for small enterprises. This chapter explores a pivotal strategy that has the potential to reshape the trajectory of small businesses – the art of audience leverage and its profound impact on driving sales growth.

In an era marked by rapid digitalisation and empowered consumers, the traditional approach of chasing after new customers has undergone a transformation. Small businesses are discovering that the key to sustainable success lies within their existing customer base – a goldmine of untapped potential waiting to be harnessed. Audience leverage is the art of strategically nurturing and engaging with this captive audience, unlocking a spectrum of benefits that extend far beyond immediate sales figures.

As we embark on this chapter's exploration, we will delve deep into the multifaceted advantages that audience leverage offers to small businesses. From cultivating brand loyalty and cost-effective marketing to harnessing the power of word-of-mouth amplification and data-driven decision-making, we'll uncover the building blocks that underpin successful sales growth. By understanding and mastering these strategies, small businesses can position themselves for remarkable expansion and prosperity, forging a path that embraces both innovation and tradition.

Through the pages that follow, we will journey through real-world examples, actionable insights, and proven tactics that showcase the symbiotic relationship between audience leverage and sales growth. As the landscape of business continues to evolve, this chapter aims to equip small business owners with the tools needed to not only thrive but also excel in an environment where the most valuable asset – the audience – becomes the driving force behind sustained success – and here's why…

1. **Enhanced Customer Engagement:** Leveraging your audience allows you to establish deeper connections with your customers. By

understanding their preferences, behaviours, and needs, you can tailor your marketing messages and offerings to resonate more effectively. This personalised approach fosters a sense of loyalty, making customers feel valued and understood.

2. **Cost-Effective Marketing:** Retaining existing customers is generally more cost-effective than acquiring new ones. In fact, recent research suggests it is 5X more expensive to get new customers than it is to sell to existing ones. By tapping into your established audience, you can allocate resources more efficiently by targeting individuals who have already shown an interest in your products or services. This approach reduces customer acquisition costs and increases the potential for higher returns on investment.

3. **Word-of-Mouth Amplification:** Satisfied customers are your best advocates. Through audience leverage, you empower your existing customers to become brand ambassadors, spreading positive word-of-mouth recommendations within their networks. This organic form of promotion can significantly extend your brand's reach and credibility, leading to a broader customer base.

4. **Refined Product Development:** Engaging with your audience provides valuable insights into their evolving preferences and needs. By leveraging this knowledge, you can fine-tune your products or services to better align with market demands. This

proactive approach not only boosts customer satisfaction but also increases the likelihood of repeat business.

5. **Trust and Credibility:** An established customer base fosters trust and credibility in your brand. Existing customers who have had positive experiences are more likely to trust your offerings and recommendations. Leveraging this trust can lead to increased cross-selling and upselling opportunities, driving additional revenue streams.

6. **Data-Driven Decision Making:** Audience leverage provides access to a wealth of data and analytics. By analysing customer behaviour, preferences, and engagement patterns, you can make informed decisions about marketing strategies, product offerings, and customer communication. This data-driven approach minimises guesswork and maximises results.

7. **Long-Term Relationship Building:** Effective audience leverage is about building lasting relationships rather than focusing solely on short-term sales. Cultivating these relationships over time encourages repeat business and brand loyalty, contributing to sustainable growth and stability.

8. **Adaptation to Market Shifts:** As the market landscape evolves, your audience's preferences and behaviours may change. By consistently engaging with your audience, you can stay attuned

to these shifts and adapt your strategies accordingly. This flexibility positions your business to remain relevant and competitive in changing market conditions.

In the pages ahead, we will delve into actionable strategies for effective audience leverage. From crafting personalised content and loyalty programmes to fostering community engagement and utilising social media platforms, these tactics will empower you to tap into the full potential of your existing audience. By doing so, you will not only bolster your sales figures but also lay the foundation for sustainable growth and long-term prosperity in the modern marketplace.

Okay, let's dive into some actionable strategies for effective audience leverage that can help businesses harness the power of their existing customer base for increased sales and sustainable growth:

1. **Craft Personalised Content:** Tailor your marketing messages and content to cater to the specific interests and preferences of your audience. Utilise data analytics to segment your audience and create content that speaks directly to their needs. Personalisation enhances engagement and builds a stronger emotional connection, leading to increased loyalty and repeat purchases. We have covered personalisation in previous chapters so you should have a good understanding of what this entails and how to implement it in your own business.

2. **Implement Loyalty Programmes:** Loyalty programmes are designed to reward repeat customers and encourage their continued engagement. Offer incentives such as discounts, exclusive offers, or points-based systems that customers can redeem for future purchases. These programmes not only boost sales but also foster a sense of belonging and appreciation. You will, no doubt, have a loyalty card from a shop you frequent such as Boots, Tesco or Sainsbury's and know that they are extremely effective at keeping customers coming back.

3. **Foster Community Engagement:** Building a sense of community around your brand can create a loyal following. Create online forums, discussion groups, or social media communities where customers can interact with each other and your brand. Encourage user-generated content and facilitate conversations that revolve around shared interests and experiences. GoPro make excellent use of user-generated content by asking their customers to send in videos that they've recorded while using their products, this is then shared on their social media and website and also in their marketing materials and because the audience have created the content it is far more relevant and relatable.

4. **Utilise Social Media Platforms:** Leverage the power of social media to connect with your audience on a personal level. Engage in two-way conversations, respond to comments and

messages promptly, and share content that resonates with your audience's values. Social media platforms provide an excellent avenue for building relationships and staying top-of-mind with customers.

5. **Segmented Email Marketing:** Use email marketing campaigns to deliver targeted content and promotions to specific segments of your audience. Tailor your messages based on past purchase history, browsing behaviour, or other relevant data. Segmented emails are more likely to capture attention and convert into sales. Most email service providers offer the opportunity to segment your lists so that you can send one email to someone who favours one product and a different email to someone who favours another.

6. **Offer Exclusive Content and Previews:** Provide your existing audience with exclusive access to new products, services, or content before they're available to the general public. This not only rewards loyal customers but also generates excitement and anticipation, which can lead to increased sales upon launch.

7. **Customer Feedback and Surveys:** Regularly seek feedback from your audience to understand their needs and preferences better. Conduct surveys, polls, and feedback forms to gather insights on product improvements, customer service enhancements, and overall satisfaction. Implementing changes based on customer input

shows that their opinions matter, fostering a stronger connection and again, it will keep your products and services more relevant and relatable.

8. **Cross-Selling and Upselling:** Leverage your existing customer relationships to introduce them to complementary or higher-tier products and services. Recommend items based on their past purchases or preferences, increasing the average order value and maximising sales potential. You will have seen Amazon do this when they show you things that others have bought along with the purchase you are about to make. Watching what the big businesses do is a great way to take advantage of what their huge marketing budgets uncover so that you can do something similar and know that it works.

9. **Create User-Generated Content Campaigns:** Encourage your customers to share their experiences with your products or services through user-generated content campaigns. This can include reviews, testimonials, photos, videos, and more. User-generated content not only serves as authentic endorsements but also expands your reach as customers share their content with their networks too. I have already talked about how GoPro uses this idea to build relationships with their audience but also to keep their marketing interesting and relevant to their audience.

10. **Continuous Engagement:** Maintain an ongoing dialogue with your audience through regular

updates, newsletters, and relevant content. Consistent engagement keeps your brand fresh in their minds and nurtures a sense of loyalty over time as we covered in detail in Chapter Fourteen.

By implementing these strategies, businesses can effectively leverage their existing audience to drive sales, foster loyalty, and establish a solid foundation for sustainable growth in the competitive modern marketplace.

Here are a few real-world examples of how large brands leverage their existing customer base to increase sales:

1. **Amazon Prime Loyalty Programme:** Amazon's Prime programme is a prime example (pun intended) of customer leverage. By offering a subscription service that provides members with benefits like free shipping, exclusive access to streaming content, and early access to deals, Amazon has successfully turned regular customers into loyal Prime members. The convenience and added value of the programme encourage members to make more purchases on Amazon, effectively boosting sales and fostering customer retention.

2. **Starbucks Rewards Programme:** Starbucks' Rewards programme is designed to encourage repeat purchases. Customers earn stars for every purchase, which they can redeem for free drinks and food items. This encourages customers to visit Starbucks more frequently and spend more

on their purchases to accumulate stars. The program not only increases sales by driving customer loyalty but also gathers valuable data about customer preferences and behaviours.

3. **Apple's Ecosystem Approach:** Apple has created a seamless ecosystem that leverages customer loyalty across its range of products and services. By designing products that work seamlessly together, such as iPhones, iPads, MacBooks, and Apple Watches, Apple encourages customers to invest in multiple devices. This ecosystem approach not only increases individual product sales but also encourages cross-selling, as loyal Apple users are more likely to purchase additional Apple products and services.

4. **Nike's NikePlus Membership:** NikePlus is a membership program that offers customers exclusive benefits like early access to product launches, personalised workout plans, and rewards. By providing unique experiences and rewards to members, Nike encourages brand loyalty and higher engagement with its products. This not only leads to increased sales but also strengthens the emotional connection between customers and the brand.

5. **Coca-Cola's Personalised Marketing:** Coca-Cola leveraged its massive customer base by using personalised marketing campaigns. The "Share a Coke" campaign was a great example. Coca-Cola

printed popular names on its bottles and encouraged customers to share photos with their personalised bottles on social media. This not only drove engagement and user-generated content but also led to increased sales as customers sought out bottles with their names.

6. **Amazon Recommendations:** Amazon's recommendation system is a sophisticated example of leveraging customer data to increase sales. By analysing customers' browsing and purchase history, Amazon suggests products that are likely to interest them. This personalised approach not only enhances the shopping experience but also drives additional sales as customers discover products they might not have found otherwise.

These examples highlight how large brands strategically leverage their existing customer base to drive sales and foster long-term loyalty. By offering tailored experiences, rewards, and personalised recommendations, these brands create a positive cycle of engagement, trust, and repeat purchases.

Here are some examples of how my own clients have leveraged their current customer base:

Nick is a brand photographer. He ran a competition on Instagram where he encouraged his customers to tag him on 50 of his posts – if they completed the task they won a product photograph shoot or a personal photoshoot.

This not only encouraged his customers to look for his posts and actively engage with them but it also helped boost his reach so that his work got seen by a much larger audience.

Ali creates beautiful fashion and homewares that are aimed at those who enjoy country pursuits. She segmented her email list so that those who had historically bought more homewares got emails that promoted those and the people who had traditionally bought more of the fashion items got email promoting those. This helped her increase her conversion rates by over 40%

Luke runs a live-music and entertainment venue and put customer feedback and surveys to the test. He sent out text messages, emails and questionnaires to his customers to find out which events they enjoyed most and why and offered a 10% discount on their next visit if they responded. He had an 80% response rate and was able to fine-tune his tribute bands to those he knew would sell out.

Lisa is an author and uses her weekly newsletter to maintain an ongoing relationship with her readers and potential new audience. Her newsletters give some behind the scenes looks at what she does and how she does it, what is going on in her world and also gives them sneaky peeks of her upcoming novels. This has kept her top of her customers minds and encourages curiosity and excitement for her new projects. Her repeat sales have almost tripled as a result of this practice.

Think about your own business. What opportunities do you have to leverage your existing customers? What products or services could you add to your business to encourage more sales? How can you personalise your interaction with your customers to make them feel valued? How can you improve your consistency of contact? Write your ideas down and implement as many of them as possible.

In the realm of small business, where every decision holds significant weight, the importance of leveraging existing customers cannot be overstated. Throughout this chapter, we've explored how this strategic approach serves as a catalyst for sales growth, providing a pathway to success that aligns seamlessly with the unique challenges and opportunities faced by small businesses.

In a landscape dominated by competition and evolving consumer behaviours, small businesses often find themselves seeking ways to maximise resources and stand out. Leveraging existing customers presents an ingenious solution – one that holds the potential to transform occasional transactions into enduring relationships. As we've seen, this approach offers a myriad of benefits, from cost-effective marketing and word-of-mouth amplification to refined product development and data-driven decision making.

By nurturing a loyal customer base, small businesses forge

connections that transcend mere transactions. The trust and credibility cultivated through personalised engagement and community building yield a powerful ripple effect, creating a network of brand advocates who willingly champion their favourite businesses within their social circles. This advocacy, in turn, extends the reach of the business, resulting in increased sales opportunities and sustained growth.

In the realm of the small business, every customer interaction is a steppingstone toward building a thriving enterprise. The strategies discussed in this chapter – from crafting personalised content and loyalty programmes to fostering community engagement and leveraging social media – serve as guideposts for small business owners to navigate this journey with finesse. By embracing these approaches, small businesses can tap into the latent potential of their existing customer base, harnessing its inherent strength to elevate the business to new heights.

In the ever-evolving landscape of commerce, where adaptability is key and every customer holds the potential for long-term impact, small businesses that master the art of audience leverage are poised for exceptional growth. As we move forward, armed with the insights and strategies unveiled in this chapter, the small business owner is empowered to transform their customer relationships into an enduring force, driving sales growth and securing a prosperous future.

PART FOUR – LEVEL UP

Welcome to a concept that's about to take your business on a thrilling ride to new heights. If you've ever wondered how to go from good to great, from ordinary to extraordinary, then you're in for a treat. In the world of business, it's not just about surviving – it's about thriving, and that's where the concept of levelling up comes into play.

Imagine your business as a character in a video game. In the beginning, you're just learning the basics, fighting small battles, and gathering the tools you need. But as you progress, you realise that the true adventure lies in overcoming challenges, unlocking new abilities, and reaching higher levels. This is the essence of levelling up your business – a journey of continuous improvement and expansion that fuels growth and success.

So, why is levelling up essential for your business's growth? Think of it as the difference between treading water and riding a wave. In today's dynamic and competitive landscape, staying stagnant isn't an option. Businesses that stand still often find themselves left behind. Levelling up is the secret sauce that propels your business forward, transforming it into a force to be reckoned with.

Throughout this section of the book we'll dive into various strategies that will equip you with the tools you need to level up your business game. From harnessing innovative technologies to optimising processes, from refining your customer experience to expanding your market reach – each strategy is a steppingstone on your journey to mastery.

So, buckle up and get ready to embark on a quest for growth, excellence, and unlimited possibilities. It's time to level up and unlock your business's full potential. Are you ready to rise to the challenge? Let's dive in and discover the art of levelling up for business success.

16 Harnessing the power of innovative technology

Welcome to a chapter that's all about making technology your ultimate ally in the journey of levelling up your business. In an era where progress is marked by pixels and algorithms, embracing innovative technologies isn't just an option – it's a strategic imperative.

Imagine having a team of tireless, hyper-efficient workers at your disposal, each armed with cutting-edge tools and boundless creativity. Well, that's the magic that innovative technologies bring to the table. From automating routine tasks to unlocking new dimensions of customer engagement, technology is the cornerstone of modern business elevation.

In this chapter, we'll delve deep into the world of transformative tech, exploring how harnessing the power of innovation can amplify your business's growth potential. Whether you're a tech-savvy entrepreneur or someone who's just starting to dip their toes into the digital pool, you're about to uncover a treasure trove of insights that will reshape the way you approach business expansion.

So why is embracing innovative technologies crucial for levelling up? The answer lies in efficiency, agility, and staying ahead of the curve. In a rapidly evolving market, businesses that adapt and adopt technology not only survive – they thrive. Whether it's streamlining operations, tapping into data-driven insights, or creating unparalleled customer experiences, technology is the secret sauce that catalyses growth.

Throughout this chapter, we'll navigate through a myriad of game-changing technologies that can revolutionise the way you do business. From AI-powered analytics to the marvels of augmented reality, from e-commerce innovations to seamless automation – each technological advancement is a steppingstone towards your business's evolution.

Get ready to embrace the future, because technology isn't just an accessory – it's the engine that propels your business into new horizons of success. Are you prepared to ride the wave of innovation and seize the untapped potential it holds? Let's dive into the world of transformative tech and explore how to harness its power for unprecedented business growth.

One of the most common challenges my clients share is the time-consuming burden of administrative tasks. From invoicing to content creation and social media management, these routine tasks often divert their attention from what truly matters – serving their customers and growing their businesses.

But here's the exciting news: you can liberate yourself from this daily grind by embracing the power of automation. In today's tech-driven landscape, a myriad of apps, tools, and AI solutions are at your fingertips, ready to streamline your operations and bring back your precious time.

For instance, meet QuickBooks – a game-changer in accounting. With its seamless functionality, it empowers you to swiftly generate invoices, track payments, effortlessly upload receipts right from your phone, and even allows your accountant to stay on top of your financial affairs from afar.

Let's talk newsletters. Crafting and sending updates can now be a breeze. Using an email service provider, you design your template, drop in your monthly highlights, and set it to auto-launch on a specific date and time. It's like having a personal assistant for your communication needs.

And oh, the magic of AI in your social media strategy! Draft your message, let AI sprinkle its charm with emojis and hashtags – watch your content come alive without the fuss. Plus, I've uncovered a tool that can transform 10 casual selfies into a collection of 100 polished headshots. No more hunting for the perfect image – it's right at your fingertips I'll spill the beans on what this tool is later on, so keep reading.

Analytics? They've gone automated too. Google Analytics and social media platforms offer a wealth of data, enabling you to decode your website visitors' behaviour, track engagement, and uncover trends that truly matter.

Now, let's talk about another game-changer: Augmented Reality (AR). Imagine giving your clients a virtual tour of their dream space, showcasing before-and-after transformations in real time. From estate agents wowing prospective buyers with immersive property tours to using AR for instant customer support on social media, the possibilities are limitless. For businesses that create transformations, like interior designers or landscapers, AR is your ticket to showcasing potential impacts like never before.

Intrigued? Embrace automation and AR, and watch as they weave efficiency, engagement, and growth into your business journey. Your time is valuable – it's time to reclaim it and unleash the full potential of your small business.

When I run my challenges, I make use of a tool that asks all the questions I need to know from the participants and depending on the answer they give me they will get a specific response. They also get all the links they need to participate in the challenge, all the things they need to do before the challenge begins and all the reminders of the day's tasks and I don't have to do a single thing. The tool I use? ManyChat.

Think about your routine tasks. Write a list of all the daily activities you perform. Could any of those be automated or taken care of by AI?

Research some of the apps that you could use for your

customer relationship management, your newsletters or email campaigns, your bookkeeping, your social media, your website analytics.

Here are some real-life examples of how big businesses have leveraged automation, AI, and augmented reality to transform their operations and drive significant impact:

1. **Amazon's Automated Warehouses:** Amazon is a pioneer in warehouse automation. They use robots to navigate the vast warehouse spaces, retrieve items, and bring them to human workers for packaging. This automation has drastically improved order fulfilment speed and accuracy, enabling Amazon to handle a massive volume of orders efficiently.

2. **Netflix's Personalised Recommendations (AI):** Netflix employs AI algorithms to analyse user viewing habits and preferences. This data powers their personalised recommendation system, suggesting shows and movies that users are likely to enjoy. This has led to increased user engagement and longer subscription retention rates.

3. **Tesla's Autonomous Driving (AI):** Tesla's vehicles are equipped with advanced AI-powered self-driving capabilities. The Autopilot feature uses sensors, cameras, and AI algorithms to navigate, change lanes, and even park. While full autonomy is still being tested, this technology has paved the way for safer and more convenient

driving experiences. Even your typical family car is now able to park itself using this technology.

4. **L'Oreal's AR Beauty Try-On:** L'Oreal's "ModiFace" AR technology allows customers to virtually try on different makeup products using their smartphones or in-store AR mirrors. Customers can see how different shades and styles look on their own faces before making a purchase. This interactive experience has increased customer engagement and influenced purchasing decisions.

5. **IKEA's Furniture Placement App (AR):** IKEA's AR app lets customers visualise how furniture items would look in their own spaces before buying. Users can place virtual furniture in their rooms using their smartphone cameras. This has reduced uncertainty for customers and increased confidence in their purchases. I used this tool to plan out a whole kitchen, it was a total game-changer for me.

6. **Walmart's Inventory Management (Automation):** Walmart utilises automation to manage inventory in their distribution centres. Robots scan shelves, track inventory levels, and alert employees when restocking is needed. This has led to improved inventory accuracy and reduced out-of-stock situations.

7. **Starbucks' AI-Powered Customer Engagement:** Starbucks uses AI-driven analytics

to understand customer preferences, buying habits, and popular products. They personalise marketing campaigns and promotions based on this data, enhancing customer engagement and driving sales growth.

8. **DHL's AI-Powered Route Optimisation:** DHL uses AI algorithms to optimise delivery routes and schedules. This reduces fuel consumption, minimises delivery times, and lowers overall operational costs, resulting in improved customer satisfaction and environmental impact.

9. **Snapchat's Augmented Reality Filters:** Snapchat's AR filters overlay virtual elements onto users' real-world images and videos. Brands can create sponsored filters, allowing users to engage with their products in a fun and interactive way. This has created new advertising opportunities and increased brand awareness.

10. **Mercedes-Benz's AR Maintenance Assistance:** Mercedes-Benz introduced AR technology to assist technicians during vehicle maintenance. Technicians wear AR glasses that display virtual overlays of vehicle schematics and repair instructions. This has reduced repair times and increased accuracy.

These examples demonstrate how automation, AI, and augmented reality have become integral to business strategies, driving efficiency, enhancing customer experiences, and propelling growth for some of the world's largest companies.

Now I'm not suggesting that you rush out and invest in AR goggles or develop a robot to do your filing, but I do hope that hearing about how other organisations are utilising this technology you will be inspired to adopt some of it in your own business.

While automation, AI, and AR offer numerous benefits to small businesses, they also come with potential negative aspects that need to be considered. The information below is by no means meant to dissuade you from taking these new technologies onboard but rather to make you aware of all the cons as well as the benefits...

1. **Initial Costs:** Implementing automation, AI, or AR solutions often requires an upfront investment in technology, software, training, and infrastructure, which can strain a small business's budget.

2. **Complex Implementation:** Integrating these technologies can be complex and time-consuming, requiring specialised expertise. Small businesses may face challenges in finding the right talent to implement and manage these systems effectively.

3. **Dependency on Technology:** Relying heavily on automation, AI, or AR could make the

business vulnerable to disruptions if technical glitches, software failures, or connectivity issues occur.

4. **Loss of Personal Touch:** Automation and technology-driven interactions can sometimes lead to a loss of the personal touch that customers value in small businesses. It might weaken the customer-business relationship.

5. **Data Privacy and Security:** Automation and AI involve handling sensitive customer data. Small businesses must ensure robust data privacy measures and protection against potential breaches, which can be resource-intensive.

6. **Job Displacement:** Automation and AI can lead to the displacement of certain manual or repetitive jobs, potentially affecting the livelihoods of employees. Businesses need to address the ethical and social implications of these changes.

7. **Learning Curve:** Employees might face challenges adapting to new technologies, leading to a learning curve that can temporarily affect productivity.

8. **Overreliance on Technology:** If a small business becomes overly dependent on automated systems, it might struggle if the technology malfunctions or if employees lack the skills to perform tasks manually.

9. **Customer Resistance:** Some customers might prefer traditional interactions over AI-driven ones, and the introduction of automation could lead to resistance or dissatisfaction.

10. **Customisation Challenges:** Implementing AI or AR solutions might not be easy for every business process, leading to the risk of misalignment between technology and business needs.

11. **Inaccuracies:** While AI can analyse data, it might not always provide perfectly accurate insights, leading to incorrect decision-making if not carefully monitored.

12. **Lack of Human Touch:** In industries where human interaction is crucial, excessive reliance on automation or AI might create a perception that the business lacks a human touch.

13. **Regulatory Compliance:** Depending on the industry, there might be regulations and compliance requirements that need to be navigated when using AI, AR, or automated systems.

14. **Constant Evolution:** The technology landscape evolves rapidly, and businesses must invest in ongoing training and updates to keep up with the latest trends, which can be time-consuming and costly.

15. **Loss of Creativity:** Overreliance on automated content generation or AI-driven decision-making

might lead to a loss of human creativity and intuition in certain areas.

16. **Misinterpretation:** In the case of AR, there's a risk that customers or employees might misinterpret the augmented elements, leading to confusion or frustration.

Small businesses should carefully weigh these potential drawbacks against the benefits when deciding to implement automation, AI, or AR solutions and should develop strategies to mitigate these risks effectively.

That said, I would thoroughly recommend looking into some simple systems and tools that are going to help you do the mundane daily tasks so that you can spend your time more effectively and grow your business more efficiently.

I am delighted to share with you the ways in which I've successfully integrated automation, AI, and AR into my business endeavours. It's essential to recognise that even as a small enterprise, you can aspire to achieve significant advancements.

Automation: To streamline various aspects of my operations, I've harnessed the power of automation. This includes automating the booking of strategy calls, lead generation, and follow-ups. Additionally, I employ automation for sending emails and newsletters, as well as scheduling social media posts. A noteworthy tool in this regard is Calendly, which seamlessly integrates with

Outlook and Google calendars to prevent scheduling conflicts. For managing leads, I utilise Mailerlite and Active Campaign to create sign-up forms for my lead magnets, facilitating consistent follow-ups. Furthermore, I employ Mailerlite for my weekly emails and monthly newsletters, enabling me to draft content in advance and schedule it for optimal delivery days and times. Social media automation is now a standard feature on most platforms; however, if you find yourself on a platform without built-in scheduling capabilities, I recommend using Buffer as a reliable scheduler.

AI: Embracing artificial intelligence has been a relatively recent development in my business journey. I initially hesitated to leverage AI's capabilities as I wasn't sure how to implement it, but soon realised its potential. Presently, I use AI for editing social media posts, emails, website copy, and even during the creation of this book. It's crucial however, to exercise responsible use of AI. While it may be tempting to let AI compose your social media content entirely, it's important to maintain your unique voice and style and relying on AI to craft your website copy can lead to generic content that lacks individuality. I stress the importance of first creating your content and then utilising AI for editing and refinement as one of the main purposes of this book is to teach you to stand out in your marketing.

AR: A fascinating addition to my toolkit is augmented reality (AR), which I've incorporated to enhance my professional image. Through a service called TryitonAI, I submitted a few selfies, and they used AR technology to generate high-definition, professional headshots. Some of these images closely resemble me, while others have a more stylised (read "messed with") appearance. These AR-generated images have proven invaluable however for daily LinkedIn updates, sparing me the effort of continually producing new selfies that I would be happy to release for public consumption.

In conclusion, the key takeaway here is that you don't need to be on the scale of Amazon or Tesla to leverage these cutting-edge technologies effectively. Instead, you must discern which of these innovations align with your objectives, whether it's boosting productivity, enhancing the user experience, elevating customer satisfaction, or reducing the time spent on repetitive tasks. By thoughtfully integrating these technologies, even small enterprises can make substantial strides towards their goals while maintaining a distinctive and authentic identity.

17 leveraging your existing resources

In the journey of entrepreneurship, it's easy to get caught up in the pursuit of more—more capital, more talent, more assets. However, the true art of business mastery lies not only in acquiring new resources but in maximising the potential of the assets you already possess. This chapter explores the profound concept of leveraging your existing resources as a potent strategy for elevating your small business to new heights.

In the world of small enterprises, where every resource counts, your existing assets are akin to a hidden treasure waiting to be unearthed. Whether it's your team's unique skills, your accumulated knowledge, your loyal customer base, or even the physical space within your establishment, there exists an abundance of untapped potential waiting to be harnessed.

Through careful strategy and thoughtful execution, you can transform these assets into catalysts for growth:

- **Your Team:** By investing in their training, motivation, and empowerment, you not only enhance their productivity but also foster a culture of innovation and excellence.

- **Your Knowledge Base:** Sharing your expertise through content creation, workshops, or consultations can position you as an industry leader and attract a broader audience.

- **Your Loyal Customers:** By nurturing these relationships and encouraging referrals, you can expand your customer base and increase repeat business.

- **Your Physical Space:** Whether it's a retail store, office, or production facility, optimising your space can enhance the customer experience and operational efficiency.

We'll take a deeper dive into these opportunities later in the chapter so make sure to stay tuned.

We'll delve deep into the art of resource optimisation, unveiling strategies that will enable you to extract maximum value from what you already have at your disposal. From transforming your loyal customers into brand advocates to repurposing your knowledge to create valuable content, we'll explore a myriad of tactics that will not only enhance your business's capabilities but also foster innovation.

Moreover, as we venture into this exploration, we'll highlight the countless success stories of entrepreneurs who have leveraged their existing resources to remarkable effect. Their experiences will serve as both inspiration and practical guidance, illustrating how a keen eye for what you already possess can lead to unprecedented growth and resilience in today's competitive landscape.

So, as we embark on this chapter's journey, open your mind to the wealth that surrounds you. Get ready to uncover the extraordinary potential hidden within your grasp and discover how, by harnessing the power of your existing resources, you can pave a path towards sustainable success for your small business.

To get those entrepreneurial juices flowing, here are some of those success stories of entrepreneurs who successfully leveraged their existing resources to achieve remarkable results:

1. **Elon Musk - Tesla and SpaceX:** Elon Musk is a prime example of an entrepreneur who leveraged his existing resources in an extraordinary way. When he co-founded Tesla, he utilised his background in technology and engineering to create electric vehicles that disrupted the

automotive industry. Musk also founded SpaceX, leveraging his engineering expertise to reduce the cost of space exploration and make it more accessible.

2. **Steve Jobs - Apple Inc.:** Steve Jobs, the co-founder of Apple, leveraged his existing design sensibilities and passion for user-friendly technology to create groundbreaking products like the iPhone and iPad. He also tapped into Apple's loyal customer base to build a thriving ecosystem of interconnected devices and services.

3. **Howard Schultz - Starbucks:** Howard Schultz transformed Starbucks from a small coffee shop into a global coffeehouse chain. He leveraged the unique experience of enjoying coffee in a European-style café setting and capitalised on the coffee culture that already existed in many countries. Schultz's vision helped Starbucks become a household name worldwide.

4. **Sara Blakely - Spanx:** Sara Blakely leveraged her personal frustration with ill-fitting undergarments and her limited savings to create Spanx, a shapewear empire. She used her own ingenuity and limited resources to design a product that filled a gap in the market, ultimately becoming a billionaire businesswoman.

5. **Jeff Bezos - Amazon:** Jeff Bezos started Amazon as an online bookstore, leveraging his knowledge of e-commerce trends and consumer

behaviour. He expanded Amazon's offerings gradually, turning it into the global e-commerce and technology giant it is today. Bezos also leveraged his technological expertise to develop Amazon Web Services (AWS), a profitable subsidiary that provides cloud computing services to businesses.

6. **Mark Zuckerberg - Facebook:** Mark Zuckerberg leveraged his programming skills and understanding of social dynamics to create Facebook, initially as a platform for connecting college students. He later expanded Facebook's reach to become the world's largest social media network, with billions of users.

7. **Oprah Winfrey - Harpo Productions:** Oprah Winfrey, through her existing media platform, The Oprah Winfrey Show, leveraged her influence to establish Harpo Productions. She used her network and brand to launch a successful magazine, create a television network (OWN), and produce critically acclaimed films and documentaries.

These entrepreneurs not only recognised the resources and expertise they possessed but also had the vision and determination to leverage them to create businesses that have made a lasting impact on industries and society as a whole. Their stories serve as inspiration for aspiring entrepreneurs looking to maximise their existing resources to achieve remarkable success.

In the previous chapter we looked at introducing innovative technologies as a way of levelling up your business, in this chapter we are going to be exploring the wealth of opportunities you have already but are probably not utilising effectively. This is a good exercise for any business to do as it will highlight the potential gaps in your business systems that you can then plug and enjoy more revenue as a result.

Leveraging your current customers can be a powerful strategy to increase turnover and grow your small business. Here are some effective ways to achieve this:

1. **Customer Loyalty Programmes:** Implement a customer loyalty programme that rewards repeat business. Offer discounts, exclusive access to products or services, or points-based systems that can be redeemed for future purchases. These incentives encourage customers to return and spend more with your business.

2. **Upselling and Cross-Selling:** Train yourself, your sales and customer service teams to identify opportunities for upselling (encouraging customers to buy a higher-priced product or service) and cross-selling (offering related products or services). For example, if you run a tech store and a customer buys a laptop, suggest accessories like a case, mouse, or extended warranty.

3. **Personalised Recommendations:** Utilise customer data and purchase history to make personalised product or service recommendations. This can be done through email marketing or on your website. Amazon's "Customers who bought this also bought..." feature is a classic example of effective personalised recommendations as is Netflix's people who watched this also watched.... as we mentioned in the previous chapter.

4. **Referral Programmes:** Encourage your satisfied customers to refer friends and family by offering referral incentives. Provide discounts, freebies, or credits for each successful referral. Word-of-mouth marketing from loyal customers can significantly boost your customer base and sales and means you're doing very little extra for what can be quite a considerable boost to your turnover.

5. **Customer Feedback and Improvement:** Actively seek feedback from your customers and use their insights to improve your offerings. When customers see that you value their opinions and make changes based on their feedback, they are more likely to remain loyal and increase their spending with your business.

6. **Exclusive Previews and Early Access:** Reward your loyal customers with exclusive previews of new products or early access to sales and promotions. This makes them feel valued and

encourages them to make purchases ahead of the general public.

7. **Subscription Models:** Consider offering subscription-based services or products. Subscription models can provide a steady stream of income, and loyal customers are more likely to commit to long-term subscriptions.

8. **Frequent Buyer Discounts:** Offer discounts or rewards for customers who make frequent purchases. For example, after every fifth purchase, provide a significant discount or a free product. This can create an incentive for customers to continue buying from your business.

9. **Special Events and VIP Programmes:** Host special events or create VIP programmes exclusively for your top customers. These events can include private sales, product launches, or gatherings that make customers feel valued and appreciated.

10. **Community Building:** Create a community around your brand where customers can connect, share experiences, and support each other. Building a strong community can lead to increased loyalty and advocacy, ultimately driving more sales.

11. **Follow-Up and Engagement:** Stay in touch with your customers through email marketing, social media, or newsletters. Share valuable content, product updates, and promotions to keep

your brand top of mind and encourage repeat business.

By strategically leveraging your current customer base and focusing on building strong, long-term relationships, you can boost turnover and create a sustainable foundation for your small business's growth.

Here are some of the things I do in my own business...

Upselling and cross-selling – The Business Builder has a suite of services that are designed to encourage higher spending. The Growth Audit is £500 and will identify all the areas where you are losing sales – we can then help you plug those gaps by either joining our Mastermind £1,500 or our one-to-one mentoring programme £3,000. We also have a website building service £1,500 or a complete turnkey business option £5,000 where we do literally everything for you. We have preventative maintenance options for £120 per month and ongoing mentoring programmes for £200 so that we encourage our clients to stay with us after their initial purchase.

Referral Programmes – We offer a 10% referral fee to anyone who sends us a new lead that becomes a paying client. This encourages not only our clients, but also our leads to recommend us to other people who would benefit from our services.

Customer Feedback and Improvement – The whole S.E.L.L. System™ was developed from feedback from clients over many years. They wanted something simple, something that made sense to them and something that actually worked. We took a complicated process (marketing) and broke it down into 4 simple steps.

Subscription Models – We have clients who pay a monthly maintenance fee for us to look after their websites and put things right when they go wrong. We also have people pay a monthly fee for our ongoing mentoring service when people want ongoing accountability and expert advice.

Special Events and Programmes – I run workshops that are exclusively for clients and others that are for anyone, but clients get a huge discount when they attend.

Community Building – I use my networking groups and my LinkedIn channel to create a community and I put on monthly masterclasses where people can come and talk to me about their business problems live.

Follow up and Engagement – Well duh! I've been banging on about this since part one of this book so if you don't know how I do this by now you need to go back to the beginning and read it all again.

Leveraging your current website can be a powerful way to increase turnover for your small business. Here are some effective strategies to achieve this:

1. **Optimise for Search Engines (SEO):** Ensure that your website is search engine optimised to rank higher in search results. Use relevant keywords, create high-quality content, and improve your website's loading speed to attract more organic traffic. This is rather simplistic, and you can get experts to help you with this but even if you just do the basics, it will improve your chances of being found by your customers.

2. **E-commerce Integration:** If you're selling products, consider adding an e-commerce functionality to your website. Make the purchasing process seamless, secure, and user-friendly, and offer various payment options to accommodate your customers. Remember, the easier you make it for someone to buy from you, the more likely they are to buy.

3. **Mobile-Friendly Design:** Ensure that your website is mobile-responsive, as an increasing number of users access websites on smartphones and tablets. A mobile-friendly design can improve user experience and boost sales. It is also a Google requisite that your website is optimised for mobile and if it's not it will be severely penalised in the rankings.

4. **Clear and Compelling Calls to Action (CTAs):** Use clear and persuasive CTAs throughout your website to encourage visitors to take specific actions, such as signing up for newsletters, making a purchase, or requesting a quote.

5. **Content Marketing:** Regularly publish valuable and relevant content on your website's blog. This not only attracts organic traffic but also positions your business as an industry authority. Content can include how-to guides, informative articles, and case studies. Blogging is also a great way to boost your SEO.

6. **Email Marketing:** Collect email addresses from website visitors and use email marketing campaigns to nurture leads and convert them into paying customers. Send personalised offers, newsletters, and product updates to engage your audience.

7. **Social Media Integration:** Integrate social media sharing buttons on your website's content and product pages to encourage visitors to share your content. Social sharing can increase your website's visibility and reach a broader audience. Beware of just adding social icons for the sake of it though as you don't want to lose a website visitor to your Instagram grid and never be seen again. There are plugins that you can use that specifically encourage website sharing so make sure to add these if you want to adopt that strategy.

8. **User Reviews and Testimonials:** Display customer reviews and testimonials prominently on your website. Positive feedback builds trust and credibility, which can lead to increased conversions.

9. **A/B Testing:** Continuously test different elements of your website, such as headlines, images, and CTAs, to determine what resonates best with your audience. A/B testing helps optimise your site for higher conversion rates.

10. **Exit-Intent Pop-Ups:** Use exit-intent pop-ups to capture visitors who are about to leave your website without taking action. Offer discounts, special offers, or free resources in exchange for their contact information or a purchase.

11. **Remarketing and Retargeting:** Implement remarketing and retargeting campaigns to reach users who have previously visited your website but didn't make a purchase. Display targeted ads to remind them of your products or services. You will need to engage an expert to set this up for you as it can be tricky, and you can end up losing more money than you make.

12. **Landing Pages:** Create dedicated landing pages for specific products or promotions. These pages can be highly focused and optimised to drive conversions, such as signing up for a webinar or making a purchase.

13. **Online Chat Support:** Offer real-time online chat support on your website to assist visitors with their questions or concerns. Prompt customer support can help close sales and improve customer satisfaction. There are tools

available that enable you to do this without having to sit on your website all day.

14. **Customer Data Analysis:** Utilise website analytics tools to track user behaviour and identify areas for improvement. Understanding how visitors interact with your site can lead to more effective optimisation. Hotjar is a great tool to use to see how people use your site, which buttons they hover over or click on and other extremely useful insights.

15. **Localised Content:** If your business serves specific geographic areas, optimise your website for local SEO and include location-specific content. This can help attract local customers searching for your products or services.

By implementing these strategies and continually refining your website's performance, you can leverage your online presence to increase turnover for your small business and achieve sustained growth.

Leveraging your current premises effectively can have a significant impact on increasing turnover for your small business. Here are some examples of how to achieve this:

1. **Visual Merchandising:** If you have a physical retail store, invest in attractive and strategic visual merchandising. Arrange your products in an appealing way, use eye-catching displays, and

create themed sections to encourage customers to explore and purchase more items.

2. **Store Layout Optimisation:** Optimise your store layout to guide customers along a well-planned path. Place high-margin or popular products at eye level and strategically position impulse-buy items near checkout counters.

3. **In-Store Promotions:** Offer in-store promotions, discounts, and exclusive deals to incentivise customers to make purchases while they're at your premises. Limited time offers and loyalty programs can also be effective.

4. **Cross-Promotion:** If you share a physical space with other businesses, consider cross-promotion. Collaborate with neighbouring businesses to run joint promotions or offer bundled products or services, creating a win-win situation for all parties.

5. **Events and Workshops:** Host events, workshops, or product demonstrations in your store or on your premises. These activities can attract foot traffic, engage customers, and provide opportunities to showcase your offerings.

6. **Customer Engagement:** Train your staff to provide excellent customer service and engage with customers. A positive shopping experience can lead to repeat business and word-of-mouth referrals.

7. **Window Displays:** Use your storefront's window space creatively to grab the attention of passersby. Change window displays regularly to feature new products or seasonal promotions.

8. **Online Integration:** If you have a physical store, ensure it's integrated with your online presence. Offer options for in-store pickup of online orders and encourage customers to leave online reviews that mention their in-store experiences. Google has just introduced a new app to make this easier for your customers to do straight from their phone while still in your premises.

9. **Store Signage:** Invest in clear and appealing signage that effectively communicates your brand and offerings. Well-designed signage can attract foot traffic and make it easy for customers to find what they need.

10. **Private Events:** Consider renting out your premises for private events, parties, or meetings. This can provide an additional revenue stream and introduce new customers to your business.

11. **Community Engagement:** Engage with your local community by participating in local events, sponsoring community initiatives, or collaborating with nearby businesses. A strong community presence can lead to increased brand loyalty.

12. **Customer Feedback:** Collect and act on customer feedback to make improvements to your premises. Addressing issues and enhancing

the overall customer experience can lead to higher turnover.

13. **Seasonal Decorations:** Decorate your premises to align with seasonal holidays or events. Themed decorations can create a festive atmosphere and encourage customers to make holiday-related purchases.

14. **Product Demonstrations:** Offer product demonstrations or samples to allow customers to experience your products firsthand. This can build trust and confidence in your offerings.

15. **Interactive Displays:** Incorporate interactive displays or technologies such as touchscreens or virtual reality experiences to engage customers and provide a unique shopping experience.

By implementing these strategies and tailoring them to your specific business and premises, you can effectively leverage your physical location to increase turnover and create a more profitable and thriving small business. You will, no doubt, have seen how the bigger businesses utilise these strategies – now go and do the same.

Leveraging your current staff effectively is crucial for increasing turnover as a small business owner. Here are some examples of how to achieve this:

1. **Training and Skill Development:** Invest in ongoing training and skill development

programmes for your staff. Well-trained employees can provide better customer service, upsell products or services, and contribute to overall business growth.

2. **Cross-Training:** Cross-train your employees to perform multiple roles within the business. This ensures flexibility in staffing and allows you to efficiently allocate resources based on demand.

3. **Sales Training:** Provide sales training to your staff, emphasising the importance of upselling and cross-selling. Equip them with techniques to identify opportunities to increase sales during customer interactions.

4. **Customer Relationship Management:** Train your staff to build strong customer relationships. Encourage them to remember customer names, preferences, and purchase history, enabling personalised service that leads to repeat business.

5. **Incentives and Bonuses:** Implement performance-based incentives and bonuses to motivate your staff to achieve sales and customer service goals. Reward employees for exceeding targets and consider offering contests or recognition programmes.

6. **Customer Feedback:** Encourage your staff to gather customer feedback and insights. This information can be invaluable for identifying areas of improvement and tailoring your products or services to customer needs.

7. **Employee Suggestions:** Create a culture where employees are encouraged to share ideas for improving processes, customer experiences, or product offerings. Employee suggestions can lead to innovative solutions that boost turnover.

8. **Efficiency Improvements:** Work with your staff to identify ways to streamline processes and improve operational efficiency. This can lead to cost savings and increased profitability.

9. **Team Collaboration:** Foster collaboration and teamwork among your staff. Encourage open communication, idea sharing, and cross-functional collaboration to solve problems and drive business growth.

10. **Leadership Development:** Identify and nurture leadership potential within your staff. Promote from within whenever possible, as employees who have grown with the company are often more invested in its success.

11. **Customer Education:** Train your staff to educate customers about the value and benefits of your products or services. Informed customers are more likely to make confident purchase decisions.

12. **Upselling Techniques:** Provide your staff with upselling techniques and scripts to effectively suggest additional products or services that complement customers' purchases.

13. **Customer Retention:** Train your staff to prioritise customer retention. A loyal customer base is more likely to make repeat purchases and refer others to your business.

14. **Feedback Implementation:** Act on feedback provided by your staff. They are often closest to customer interactions and may have valuable insights into what works and what needs improvement.

15. **Recognition and Appreciation:** Show appreciation for your staff's hard work and dedication. Recognise outstanding performance and celebrate achievements to boost morale and motivation.

16. **Flexible Scheduling:** Offer flexible work schedules or remote work options when feasible. This can help retain valuable employees and improve their work-life balance, leading to increased job satisfaction and productivity.

By harnessing the skills, knowledge, and dedication of your current staff, you can create a motivated and efficient workforce that contributes significantly to increasing turnover and the overall success of your small business.

And finally, one of my favourite ways to level up a business – Creating Passive Income Streams...

Leveraging passive income streams can be a valuable strategy for increasing turnover as a small business owner. Here are some examples of how to achieve this:

1. **Affiliate Marketing:** Partner with other businesses and promote their products or services through affiliate marketing on your website or social media channels. Earn a commission for each sale generated through your referral links.

2. **Dropshipping:** Integrate dropshipping into your e-commerce business model. This allows you to sell products without holding inventory. When customers make purchases, the products are shipped directly from suppliers, reducing your operational overhead.

3. **Digital Products and E-books:** Create and sell digital products, such as e-books, online courses, templates, or downloadable resources, through your website. Once created, these products can generate revenue without ongoing production costs.

4. **Subscription Models:** Offer subscription-based services or products. Subscribers pay a recurring fee for access to exclusive content, products, or ongoing services, providing a predictable income stream.

5. **Membership Sites:** Create a membership site with premium content or services that users must subscribe to access. Charge a monthly or yearly

fee for membership, providing continuous income as long as members remain active.

6. **Ad Revenue:** If you have a high-traffic website or blog, monetise it by displaying relevant advertisements. Platforms like Google AdSense can help you earn passive income through ad clicks and impressions. Be careful though, as too many adverts popping up on your website can detract from your main offers, confuse visitors and lead to less revenue.

7. **Rental Income:** If you own physical assets or properties, consider renting them out when not in use. This can include renting office space, equipment, or even unused storage space.

8. **License Your Intellectual Property:** If you hold patents, trademarks, or copyrights, license these intellectual property rights to other businesses in exchange for royalties. This can be particularly lucrative in industries like software, music, or publishing.

9. **Investment Income:** Invest surplus business profits in stocks, bonds, real estate, or other income-generating assets. Earnings from investments can provide a consistent source of passive income.

10. **Franchising:** If your business model is replicable, consider franchising it to others who want to operate their own locations under your brand.

Franchise fees and ongoing royalties can create a stream of passive income.

11. **Peer-to-Peer Lending:** Invest in peer-to-peer lending platforms where you can lend money to individuals or small businesses in exchange for interest payments. This can be a source of passive income with potential returns. Zopa is an example of a peer-to-peer lending company.

12. **Real Estate Crowdfunding:** Participate in real estate crowdfunding platforms that allow you to invest in real estate projects with a relatively small capital commitment. Earn rental income or a share of profits from property appreciation.

13. **Dividend Stocks:** Invest in dividend-paying stocks. Companies that distribute a portion of their profits as dividends can provide regular, passive income through dividend payouts.

14. **Royalties from Artistic Work:** If you're an artist, writer, musician, or content creator, earn royalties from your work's licensing, streaming, or sales. Platforms like Spotify, Kindle Direct Publishing, and others offer opportunities for royalty income.

15. **Automated Online Businesses:** Create and automate online businesses, such as dropshipping stores, affiliate marketing websites, or content-driven blogs. These can generate passive income with minimal ongoing effort.

I started my whole online marketing journey through

passive income. Remember my swimming goggles from Chapter Three? I sold many pairs of goggles by creating just one blog post that sent viewers to my Amazon listing and I sold my goggles on the back of that one post for about six years.

Having learned the power of the blog post I then became an affiliate marketer and sold other people's products and services for a commission.

Remember that building passive income streams often requires an initial investment of time, resources, or capital. It's essential to choose passive income opportunities that align with your business's strengths, resources, and long-term goals. Additionally, diversifying your passive income sources can help protect against financial risks and enhance your overall turnover.

In the pursuit of growth and success as a small business owner, the world often presents itself as an endless quest for more resources, more capital, more customers. However, as we've explored in this chapter, there is a profound and often overlooked wellspring of potential right at your fingertips: what you already have.

We've delved into the art of leveraging your current resources to increase turnover, recognising that in the world of small enterprises, where every asset is precious, your existing foundation can be your greatest advantage.

From the skills and dedication of your team to the wealth of knowledge accumulated over time, from your loyal customer base to the very physical space you occupy— these are the building blocks of your business's success.

Through careful strategy and thoughtful execution, you can transform these assets into catalysts for growth:

- **Your Team:** By investing in their training, motivation, and empowerment, you not only enhance their productivity but also foster a culture of innovation and excellence.

- **Your Knowledge Base:** Sharing your expertise through content creation, workshops, or consultations can position you as an industry leader and attract a broader audience.

- **Your Loyal Customers:** By nurturing these relationships and encouraging referrals, you can expand your customer base and increase repeat business.

- **Your Physical Space:** Whether it's a retail store, office, or production facility, optimising your space can enhance the customer experience and operational efficiency.

Throughout this journey, we've seen that the ability to innovate, adapt, and leverage your existing resources is the hallmark of a thriving small business. It's not about having more; it's about making the most of what you have.

As you move forward, I encourage you to embrace this mindset of resourcefulness. Continue to explore new ways to leverage your existing assets creatively and remember that the journey of entrepreneurship is not just about the destination but the path you take to get there. By maximising the potential of what you already possess, you can build a sustainable and prosperous future for your small business—one that's anchored in the strength of your foundations and the boundless possibilities they offer.

18 putting it all together.

Throughout this remarkable journey of discovery spanning 17 enlightening chapters, we have explored the transformative impact of making nuanced adjustments to your business practices. The profound implications of these refinements on your business's trajectory have unfolded before us.

Now, as we approach the culmination of this voyage, it is natural to sense a certain overload of information and wonder where or how to commence the implementation process, especially as you have, no doubt, experienced unfamiliar ideas and concepts along the way. In this final chapter, we shall demystify the transition from knowledge to action, distilling it into four straightforward steps.

Step 1: Stand Out

To distinguish yourself from competitors, consider how you can capture your audience's attention and imprint your brand in their consciousness. This doesn't mean you have to go to extravagant measures but rather thoughtful strategies to ensure you stay in your customers' minds ahead of your competitors.

Step 2: Engage

In the contemporary landscape, simply promoting your business isn't enough. Flourishing businesses actively engage with their audiences, crafting immersive experiences that foster enduring connections. Contemplate diverse methods to engage your audience, both in the digital realm and through real-world interactions.

Step 3: Leverage

The ability to convert leads into loyal customers is the linchpin of success for every enterprise. Construct captivating lead magnets that resonate with your audience and orchestrate a nurturing process that culminates in their decision to invest in your offerings.

Step 4: Level Up

The time is ripe to examine the myriad ways in which you can leverage your existing assets to elevate your business. Exploit every opportunity and harness all available resources to catalyse growth.

These four steps form the foundation of the S.E.L.L. System™ methodology, which has empowered the growth and scalability of over 3,000 small businesses to date. Whether you opt to embark on one step at a time or enthusiastically initiate all four is entirely at your discretion. Our only counsel is to take action, no matter how small the initial step may be.

Overwhelm is a familiar companion when contemplating marketing endeavours. By distilling the process into these four fundamental steps, my aim is to simplify your journey, rendering it more manageable and less likely to be relegated to the back burner.

My intention throughout this book has been to empower you with actionable insights. Now that you have glimpsed the potential that lies ahead, I hope you will approach the application of these lessons with enthusiasm and the conviction that remarkable transformations await.

However, it is possible that you may seek some guidance to initiate your journey. Recognising this need, I understand that having a clear understanding of what steps to take is crucial in the process of taking action. Therefore, the remainder of this chapter is dedicated to actionable ideas that you can promptly implement to foster the growth of your business starting today.

Standing Out

social media: Commit to a daily posting regimen on your social media platforms. Consider what sets your business apart and infuse that uniqueness into your content. For instance, I often employ humour to amuse and engage my audience, aligning with the ethos of The Business Builder, where we find fun in business building.

What to Post:

- Share your business journey, including why you embarked on this venture, your aspirations for your customers, obstacles encountered, and the strategies employed to overcome them.

- Showcase customer testimonials by presenting them as engaging images along with the client's feedback. Use these testimonials as the foundation for your posts, elaborating on how your business provided value.

- Offer case studies to illustrate how your products or services have helped clients achieve their goals or fulfil specific needs.

- Share videos featuring your products or services or engage with your audience through informative videos where you explain your offerings.

- Utilise Instagram Reels for concise video clips.

- Don't forget to highlight special offers to keep your audience informed.

Networking: Dedicate yourself to attending at least one in-person networking event each month. Take the opportunity to build meaningful connections with fellow attendees.

Gifts and Freebies: Deliberate on simple and cost-effective tokens to offer individuals you meet. For instance, I provide chocolates, superhero badges, a motivational card, and brand-coloured pens. These thoughtful gestures cost approximately £2 but leave a lasting impression. Avoid overt promotional materials such as pens with your phone number, as this goes against the spirit of genuine connection.

Engaging
Workshops: Organise workshops, which can be conducted online at no cost or offline with a nominal fee to cover venue expenses. Leverage these workshops as a platform to showcase your products or services, enabling attendees to better comprehend your offerings.

Networking (Post-Event): Following networking events, send emails to contacts from those you received business cards. Express your gratitude for them talking to you and offer them the chance to talk more about their business by perhaps meeting for a coffee.

Online Groups: Explore relevant groups on platforms like Facebook and LinkedIn, where you can engage in discussions with like-minded individuals and potential future customers. Some networking groups also maintain their own online communities, so be sure to enquire and, if available, join them.

Leveraging

Lead Magnets: Craft enticing lead magnets that resonate with your target audience, encouraging them to sign up. Promote these lead magnets through your social media posts and provide links for sign-ups.

Nurture Series: Establish an automated welcome nurture series that follows the delivery of your lead magnet. This series maintains ongoing communication and engagement. Services such as Mailerlite offer a free platform to set up this nurturing sequence.

Levelling   Up

Referral Incentives: Implement straightforward referral incentives that reward those who bring new customers to your business. These incentives can be as simple as monetary rewards per lead or offering a free coaching session or a discount voucher for their next purchase.

Passive Income: Explore avenues to transform aspects of your business into passive income streams. Consider renting out unused space, creating informative "how-to" guides, or producing video tutorials. Platforms like YouTube offer free hosting for your videos, while Zoom provides free recording capabilities for sessions lasting up to 40 minutes.

Incorporating these strategies requires only a modest investment of time and patience, with no additional financial burden.

Throughout this book, my intention has been to equip you with actionable insights. Now, having glimpsed the potential that lies ahead, I hope you will approach the application of these lessons with enthusiasm and the conviction that remarkable transformations await.

As you contemplate the next steps in your journey, remember that immediate action is the catalyst for growth. The strategies presented here require nothing more than a bit of your time and patience. The quicker you implement them, the faster your business will grow and flourish.

So, with the knowledge you've acquired, and the practical guidance provided, we encourage you to take those initial steps today and watch your business thrive. Your potential for success is boundless, and the path to achieving it starts now.

Conclusion: Unlocking the Future with the S.E.L.L. System™

As we reach the final pages of this book, we stand at the threshold of an exciting future—a future where your small business has the potential to rise above the ordinary, to flourish, and to create a lasting impact.

Throughout these pages, we've embarked on a journey together, exploring the S.E.L.L. System™ methodology and the four pivotal steps it encompasses: Standing Out, Engaging, Leveraging, and Levelling Up.

In our quest to stand out, we've discovered that the essence of differentiation lies in capturing the hearts and minds of your audience. It's not about extravagant measures but rather the art of thoughtful strategies that ensure your brand remains indelibly etched in the memories of your customers.

Our exploration of engagement has revealed that in today's business landscape, promotion alone is no longer sufficient. Flourishing businesses are those that forge authentic connections, crafting immersive experiences that transcend the transactional and nurture enduring relationships. We've delved into diverse methods of engaging your audience, both in the digital realm and through the richness of real-world interactions.

The cornerstone of our journey, leveraging, has taught us the significance of transforming leads into loyal customers. It's the alchemy of creating compelling lead magnets that resonate with your audience, coupled with the orchestration of nurturing processes that guide them toward investing in your offerings.

Lastly, our endeavour to level up has unveiled the myriad ways in which you can harness the full potential of your existing assets to elevate your business. The opportunities are limitless, and by seizing every chance and optimising every resource, you can catalyse growth and innovation.

The S.E.L.L. System™ methodology has served as your compass throughout this voyage, guiding you toward a brighter, more prosperous future. Its principles have empowered countless small businesses to achieve growth, scalability, and success. Whether you choose to implement one step at a time or embrace all four with fervour, taking action is the catalyst for your journey's next phase.

As you close the final chapter and turn your attention to the horizon of possibilities, remember that your potential for success is boundless. The path to achieving it starts with the knowledge you've acquired and the practical guidance you've received. Now, it's your turn to take those initial steps, to implement what you've learned, and to witness your small business flourish.

The future is yours to shape, and with the S.E.L.L. System™ as your ally, there are no limits to what you can achieve. As you embark on this exciting new chapter, do so with enthusiasm, confidence, and the unwavering belief that remarkable transformations await. Your journey has just begun, and the best is yet to come.

ABOUT THE AUTHOR

Hi there, I'm Lynne Thomas and I'm the one who's been talking to you throughout these pages. I'm not usually so professional or eloquent when I talk to my clients, but as I wanted this book to be available to people who maybe haven't met me yet, I thought the more traditional approach to writing was more appropriate.

But now let's dive into getting to know the REAL me…

For as long as I can remember I've wanted to teach and train. Picture this: as a kid, I'd set up my makeshift classroom right in the kitchen, balancing a blackboard precariously between two doorknobs. My budding teaching career hit a snag when that blackboard decided to take a nosedive, giving an unsuspecting kitchen chair quite a surprise by breaking it in two. My mom very quickly stepped in and put a stop to my kitchen classroom.

At 19 I became a civilian instructor for the RAF's local Cadet squadron and taught Principles of Flight – so if you ever wondered how an aeroplane stays up, I'm ya girl!

I got married in my 20's and had two wonderful boys, Martyn and Chris. Chris works with me in The Business Builder, he is the one that codes the websites and makes your motion graphics etc. Martyn is the practical one and can do literally anything in DIY – how lucky am I?

Fast forward a bit, and my management career had me championing training and personal development for my staff. Then, in my 40s, I decided to take on a psychology degree, proudly earning letters after my name BScPsych(hons), or at least I think that's what they are as it's been so long since I've used them.

After leaving a long career in retail management I retrained as an NVQ assessor – and loved it, it played to all my strengths and I relished being able to help people achieve what was, for some, their first ever qualification. I then added functional skills tutor to my list of qualifications and taught English, Maths and IT to those who were taking the full NVQ qualification.

After a few years things changed, as they often do. Ofsted became too influential in how the NVQ's were delivered and it became less vocational and more academic. It also meant that ticking boxes was far more important than seeing candidates and spending time with them teaching and training them in new skills. Assessors began leaving the profession and those of us who were left were given larger and larger caseloads.

After a while I became ill. My body staged a full-blown revolt, with joints seizing up from my toe knuckles to my neck. Doctors subjected me to every test in the medical playbook, only to deliver an unexpected diagnosis: stress. That was the push I needed for some major changes.

I looked around for something to do from home. I

wanted to work at home, on my own, in my pajamas and not have to worry about commuting for two or three hours every day. I wanted to find something to do where I wasn't beholden to anyone else. I wanted more control over my life and the hours I worked.

Scouring the vast expanse of the internet for new opportunities, I dreamt of a life free from epic commutes and the corporate straitjacket. And then, in one of those serendipitous online scrolls, I stumbled upon a guy pedaling his way through the Indian Ocean. This guy was talking about online marketing and how it had helped him become financially free, he talked about being able to sell anything to anyone anywhere in the world – and that really sparked my imagination.

I eagerly signed up for his free 5-day video series, and by the third day, I found myself enrolling in his mentoring programme. Little did I know that was the day my world would change forever.

I spent the next three years learning everything there was to know about online marketing. It was a journey that saw me mastering the art of building websites, unveiling the secrets of effective social media strategies, crafting captivating content, orchestrating pay-per-click ad campaigns, and engineering lead generation and conversion systems that operated on autopilot. Each day was a new chapter, a new adventure into the digital realm.

As part of my training, I had to pick a product to sell, you will remember this from chapter three in the book, swimming goggles emerged as my choice, a product dear to my heart as I am a swimmer. Little did I know then that this choice would teach me a profound lesson in the art of niching down and focusing on selling the benefit of the product rather than its features.

After a while my confidence grew and I added new products to my line. Ear plus, skipping ropes, yoga mats, massage balls and other things I came across along the way (but boy do I wish I had got in on the fidget spinner craze).

I then learnt about affiliate marketing, a revelation that transformed my approach entirely. Now, I didn't need to create, buy, or manage products myself. Instead, I became a seller of others' creations, earning commissions for every sale I facilitated. It was a game-changer, a turning point in my new home-based career.

I was now living my dream, sitting at home in my pajamas selling things online to people all over the world. It was my dream come true. Yet, the dream didn't unfold exactly as I had envisioned. Something crucial was missing - I yearned for human connection, for a life beyond the confines of my home office. The solitude was taking its toll, and I knew it was time for a change. So, I got busy and came up with a cunning plan...

I contacted a charity that I had once worked for who helped people into self-employment. I asked if their clients would like some free training on how to market their businesses online. They welcomed my offer with open arms, and I delivered 3 workshops which they loved, their clients loved, and they asked me if I would make it a permanent thing. I ran those workshops 3 times a month for almost three years – and that's how my current business was born.

I then got asked if I would mentor some of their clients as part of their funding agreements and I was only too pleased to accept as this gave me an additional income stream (which now made 3). Things went well for about two years and then came an unexpected twist. Like a balloon that had swelled to its limit, the bubble burst on January 17th, 2017.

I had just returned from a holiday when I received an email from the charity, a message that would change the course of my story. Their funding had run dry, and they could no longer afford my services. In an instant, I had lost all of my clients and I wasn't sure how I was going to compensate for the loss in income that I had come to rely on.

But like most setbacks, it taught me a lesson – don't rely on other people for your clients. I made up my mind to go out and find my own clients. I took on a training room in a local area and with the arsenal of marketing skills I'd imparted to others, I promoted my own free workshops, cleverly crafted as lead magnets.

Those workshops turned out to be more than a beacon for potential clients; they were the keys to lasting connections. Attendees soon became valued clients, some of whom remain loyal patrons to this day. I even made friends along the way, like the one who nagged me into writing this very book.

Life was sailing smoothly. My mentoring programmes, masterminds, and masterclasses were drawing eager participants, and my bank balance was on the mend. The future appeared bright, full of promise.

And then the pandemic hit.

Fortunately, my expertise in online marketing and two other online income streams, selling swimming goggles and affiliate marketing, shielded me from the worst of the storm. I not only continued to support my clients over Zoom, a novelty to many at the time, but I also stepped up to provide training for the Chamber of Commerce and the local council, where other trainers feared to tread.

In 2020, my partner and I decided to embark on a new chapter, bidding farewell to the old locale and setting our sights on a fresh beginning. I closed my trusty training room, envisioning a new one in Worcester where we were intending to settle. Little did I know what awaited me in the shadows. In March 2021, I received a diagnosis that sent shockwaves through my world: Breast Cancer.

As you can imagine, my world crumbled, and my business

took a back seat. The ensuing months were a bit of a blur, but my spirit remained unbroken. With the kind of cancer I had, there was hope, and after surgery and radiotherapy, I was given the all clear. But the hiatus had taken its toll, and I found myself facing the uphill climb of starting over, with no local relationships to rely on for referrals or anyone to help me build my business back up.

2022 became a year of struggle. My online ventures sustained me to some extent, but the Amazon marketplace, once a reliable source of income, had become prohibitively expensive. Acquiring new clients was also an uphill battle in my new hometown, where I was a stranger to all.

Then came the turning point in 2023—a year of transformation. I decided to embrace change with open arms. I joined local networking groups, not merely as a passive member but as an engaged participant. I seized every opportunity for one-on-one meetings, forming new friendships and fostering collaborations. My business underwent a remarkable rebranding, shedding its old skin for a vibrant, fun-filled persona, and Chris, my son, agreed to get on board and add his unique skills and talent to the mix.

So far, this year has been fruitful, and I celebrated my best month ever, and I eagerly anticipate an even brighter 2024—a year that promises to be my best yet. The path ahead is uncertain, but one thing remains unwavering— my spirit, fuelled by resilience and a passion for helping others succeed.

To date I have helped over 3,000 small business owners to build, grow and scale businesses through my free workshops and challenges, my masterminds and masterclasses, my mentoring programme and our new addition - The Turnkey Solution, where we do everything for you.

I am so pleased and proud to have been able to help in some way towards these businesses' success, but also in supporting the dreams and ambitions of their owners.

I sincerely hope that this book will go some way to helping you achieve your dreams and goals too and I thank you for spending your valuable time with me here.

Lynne x

If you would like to learn more about what we do please visit thebusinessbuilderonline.com.

Printed in Great Britain
by Amazon

31962282R00155